AMERICA'S

Q·U·I·L·T·S

CREATED BY THE COUNTRY'S BEST QUILTERS

PUBLICATIONS INTERNATIONAL, LTD.

CARVAJAL S.A.
Impreso en Colombia
Printed in Colombia

ISBN 0-88176-960-6

Library of Congress Catalog Card Number: 90-83417

Photo Credits

Jennifer Amor Designs©: 24, 25; **AP/WideWorld Photos:** 17; **Jay Bachemin:** 160, 161; **Bryan Bauer:** 66; **Clinton Bell:** 67; **Sue Benner:** 32, 33; **Jan Bindas:** 94, 95; **Richard A. Brown:** 172, 173; **Tafi Brown:** 34, 35; **Trey Cambern:** 70, 71; **David Caras:** 30, 31, 44, 45, 140, 141; **Joyce Marquess Carey:** 40, 41, 42, 43; **John Corriveau:** 159; **Denver Art Museum:** 116, 117, Back Cover (middle left); **Chris Wolf Edmonds:** 52, 53, 54, 55; **eeva-inveri:** 157; **Michael Faeder:** 96, 97, 154, 155, 156, 157, Back Cover (lower right); **Ann Fahl:** 57; **Caryl Bryer Fallert:** 58, 59, 60, 61; **Marianne Fons:** 62, 63; **Curtis Fukuda:** 110, 111, 112, 113, Back Cover (lower center); **Gregory Gantner:** 20, 153; **G.E. Garrison:** 163; **Dennis Griggs:** 88, 89; **Robert Hall:** 73; **Barbara Oliver Hartman:** 74, 75; **Mary Kay Hitchner:** 80, 81; **Michael Houghton/STUDIOHIO:** 86, 87; **Damaris Jackson:** 84, 85; **Michael Keefe:** 168, 169; **Helen King:** 91; **Erik Landsberg:** 104, 105, 106, 107, Back Cover (lower right); **David Lutrell Photography/*Quilts of Tennessee:*** 5, 6, 7, 8, 9, 11, 13, 14, 15, 18, 19; **David Lutrell Photography/Marikay Waldvogel Collection:** Front Cover (lower right), 13, 16; **John Maccanelli:** 56; **Jan Maher:** 100, 101; **Nelson Malwitz:** 102, 103; **Jack Mathieson:** 77, 108, 109, Back Cover (middle center); **McCord Museum of Canadian History:** 5; **Margaret J.**

Miller: 114, 115; **John Morser/Pat Brooks Gaska:** 65; **Museum of American Folk Art:** 10; **Museum of Fine Arts Boston:** 191; **Sam Newbury:** 122, 123; **Velda E. Newman:** 128, 129; **Noho Gallery, New York:** 184, 185, 187; **Lindsay Olsen:** 138, 139; **Photography Unlimited:** 159; **Greg Plachta:** 72, 76; **Sharon Risedorph:** Front Cover (upper left), 98, 99, 124, 125, 158, 162, 163, Back Cover (upper right); **Stephanie Santmyers:** 150, 151; **Terry Schank:** Front Cover (upper right), 152; **Paul Schmorrow:** 93; **Shelbourne Museum:** 7; **Siede/Preis Photography:** Front Cover (lower left), 21, 22, 23, 26, 27, 28, 29, 36, 37, 38, 39, 50, 51, 63, 64, 68, 69, 78, 79, 82, 83, 90, 118, 119, 120, 121, 126, 127, 130, 131, 142, 143, 144, 145, 146, 147, 148, 149, 165, 166, 167, 170, 171, 176, 177, 178, 179, 182, 183, Back Cover (upper center, upper left, middle right); **Silver Dollar City:** 77; **Lois Tornquist Smith:** 164, 165; **Eric Torgersen:** 92, 93; **Meiny Vermaas-van der Heide:** 174, 175; **Ken Wagner:** 136, 137; **Marikay Waldvogel:** 4; **Jan C. Watten:** 132, 133, 134, 135; **Louise Webber:** 141; **Mark Weinkle and Greg Plachta Photography/ North Carolina Quilt Project:** 12; **Sarah Wells:** 21, 46, 47; **Carol D. Westfall:** 180, 181; **Gayle Willson Gallery:** 186; **Young Masters Studio/Judy B. Dales:** 48, 49; **Emily Zopf:** 188, 189.

◆ TABLE OF CONTENTS ◆

Quiltmaker unknown, Log Cabin in Squares and Diamonds, *circa 1870; 77¼ by 95¾ inches; wool; hand pieced.*

QUILTMAKING IN AMERICA

Overlapping layers of the rich cultural, aesthetic, and artistic heritage of our country are stitched into America's quilts. The history of quiltmaking flows with the current of the nation's economy, reflects the political environment, and echoes the drama of national and international crises. Quilts have never been simple, utilitarian bed covers; too much time and imagination goes into making a quilt for its function to take precedence over its creative form.

A pragmatic observer might expect that sewing machines, inexpensive blankets, or central heat would have brought about the demise of quiltmaking. But the art of quiltmaking has endured, and quilters have managed to find time to make quilts no matter how much their lives have changed since the first American quilts were made during colonial times. Today's fabric artists are not surprised to find that they have a lot in common with both quiltmakers of the past and also with the skilled needlewoman who sits in front of her television set carefully making a quilt for her new grandchild.

The story of America, particularly of American women, is told with quilts, but it is the look and feel of America's quilts that make them the treasured blending of art and craft that people in this country have enjoyed for generations. For quilters themselves quiltmaking is precious time spent with friends; it is creative time; and it is never seen as a waste of time. A finished quilt is always cherished and often shared; it is a reflection of what is best about American life—caring, skill, and ingenuity.

Quiltmaking Basics

Quiltmaking has remained essentially the same since colonial times. Styles, fabrics, and tools have changed, but quiltmaking continues to be a process that is easily learned from your mother, grandmother, or friend. The basics of quiltmaking are simple, but getting beyond the basics takes this craft quickly into the kind of personal expression usually thought of as art. A quilt is simply two layers of fabric with batting between that are stitched or tied together. There are three steps involved in completing a quilt: constructing the outer layers, called the quilt top and the lining, or back; sandwiching the two outer layers with batting and joining them securely; and finishing.

To make a quilt top, a quiltmaker creates or chooses a design; finds appropriate fabric; makes cutting patterns, or templates, from paper, tin, or sandpaper; marks the fabric; cuts out the pieces; and sews them together. If the quiltmaker sews pieces of fabric with the right sides together, the process is called piecing. If the quiltmaker sews pieces of fabric onto a background cloth, hemming down the edges, the process is called appliqué. Many quilts include a combination of the two methods. Crazy Quilt and Log Cabin patterns are made with press piecing,

Quiltmaker unknown, Yankee Puzzle, *1726; dimensions not available; silk; hand pieced.*

Iora Almina Philo Pool, Sampler of Blocks, *circa 1870; 83 by 75½ inches; cotton; hand pieced.*

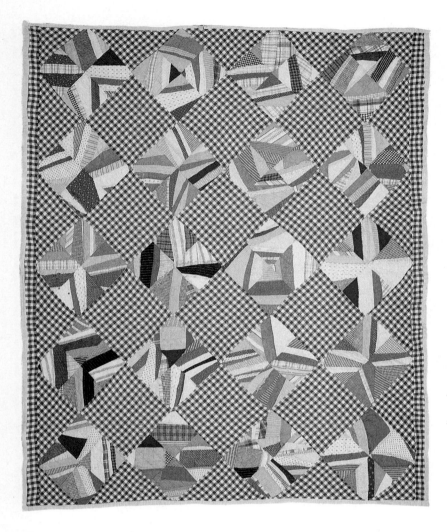

Florence Ellen LaFollette, String Quilt, *1920; 59½ by 70½ inches; cotton; hand pieced and hand quilted.*

Blanche Hurst Pangle, Pig Pen Log Cabin *(detail), circa 1910; 82 by 58 inches; silk; hand pieced and hand tied.*

which means that the block is sewn onto a cloth foundation. String piecing is similar except that the pieces are sewn onto a paper foundation. The quilt-maker makes a block by stitching one piece right side up to the center of the foundation block. The next piece is laid right side down on the first piece, and the quiltmaker stitches through both the foundation cloth and the first quilt piece along one edge. The second piece is folded back and finger pressed in place. The next piece is sewn onto the second piece, and the process continues until the foundation is completely covered. If the foundation is paper, it is usually removed before quilting begins. A whole-cloth quilt has a top that is made only of lengths of the same solid-color fabric sewn side by side. This kind of quilt shows off quilting to its fullest advantage.

Quilt linings are made of lengths of solid-color cloth, calico, or even chintz. Recently, some quiltmakers have revived the art of making two-sided quilts, with pieced or appliquéd designs on both the top and back. To join the two sides, the quiltmaker attaches the quilt back to four sides of a quilting frame and spreads out a fluffy batting of cotton or wool on the tightly stretched lining. The quilt top goes over the batting, and the quiltmaker bastes the layers together. Tying is the quickest way to permanently join the layers. The quiltmaker simply knots heavy thread or string at regular intervals across the quilt. Some quilters hide the knotted ends on the back of their quilts; others embellish them with beads or yarn balls. Quilting is a better and much more beautiful way of holding a quilt together. The quilter inserts small running stitches through the three layers in a pattern that can be as intricate as stipple quilting or as simple as straight lines. Fan quilting, diamond quilting, and quilting by the piece (or in the ditch) are other popular utilitarian quilting patterns. Some quilters draw quilting lines on the quilt top with chalk or pencil or by pulling a needle across the fabric, some eyeball the quilting pattern, and others use stamping paste with quilting stencils, made of tin or cardboard, to transfer intricate traditional designs.

When the last quilting stitch is tied off, the quiltmaker removes the quilt from the frame and finishes the edges. Quilters in the nineteenth century added straight binding around the quilt to cover the rough edges. Other finishing methods include simply folding excess lining fabric over the edges and sewing it along the front, sometimes with the addition of inset cording or attached fringe. When bias binding was introduced in the early-twentieth century, quiltmakers began to scallop the edges of their quilts because the binding allowed for easier finishing of a rounded edge.

English Roots of America's Quilts

By the beginning of the eighteenth century, the American colonies had a fairly stable economy and imported fabric for dressmaking and quiltmaking. Many American women had the time and money to make quilts, and following the example of their English counterparts, they usually made whole-cloth quilts, cutout chintz appliquéd quilts, or template-pieced hexagon quilts. Unlike many distinctly American quilts these quilt designs are organized around a large central medallion.

Whole-cloth quilts made of silk or glazed linsey-woolsey are the direct descendants of the quilted petticoats that were fashionable until the early 1800s. These underskirts filled in the opening at the front of the skirt just below the waist of the dress. After the fashion died out, seamstresses opened out old petticoats and pieced them together to make quilts. Some quilters also transferred the intricate designs they had used on underskirts to whole-cloth quilts. By 1840 this kind of quilt was no longer made in New England, but in the South quiltmakers continued to add elaborate quilting and trapunto to white areas in both their appliquéd and pieced quilts.

Cutout chintz appliquéd quilts are arranged around a central medallion. Quilters cut out floral or bird motifs from colorfully printed chintz fabrics imported from England and appliquéd them to an off-white background. They framed their arrangements with borders of colorful imported block printed fabric. The charm of cutout chintz appliqué, also known as *broderie perse*, is that each quiltmaker was able to create a unique design by rearranging the printed motifs. As chintz appliqué became more popular, textile designers, such as John Hewson, began to produce printed square panels appropriate for Medallion quilts.

To make a template-pieced quilt, a quilter must cut out thousands of hexagons from paper and the same number of slightly larger hexagons from fabric. The quilter covers each paper hexagon with a cloth hexagon and bastes the edges of the cloth to the paper from the back side. To assemble the quilt top, the quilter places two cloth-covered hexagons right sides together and using an overhand stitch joins the two hexagons on one edge. The paper templates allow for accurate, tight seams and stitches that can be nearly invisible. Template-pieced quilts have never been as popular in the United States as they are in England. But string piecing, which also uses a paper foundation, became popular with American quiltmakers during the last quarter of the nineteenth century.

America's Own Quilt Styles

By 1850 uniquely American styles of quiltmaking had eclipsed British Medallion quilts, and quilters were using multiple blocks of equal size for both pieced and appliquéd quilts. They were also creating their own appliqué designs, replacing cutout chintz appliqués with designs made up of individual components. Instead of cutting out a picture printed on cloth, American quiltmakers created their own appliquéd blocks by arranging pieces of fabric on a background to make pictures or designs. An appliquéd quilt can be as simple as four large blocks or as elaborate as a Baltimore Album quilt with dozens of intricately designed blocks.

Quiltmaker unknown, Chintz Appliquéd Quilt, *1825; dimensions not available; cotton; hand quilted.*

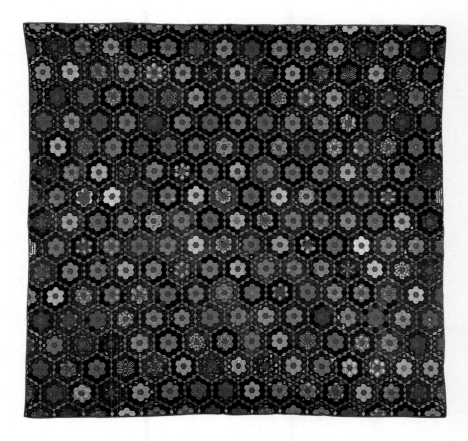

Eliza Benton Boyles Bagley, Martha Washington's Flower Garden, *1860; 90³⁄₄ by 85 inches; wool; hand pieced in the English template method and hand quilted.*

Ann Catharine King, Whig Rose, *1850; 76 by 91 inches; cotton; hand pieced and hand quilted.*

Kate McNabb Wood, Rose of Sharon, *1860; 83 by 91 inches; cotton; hand pieced and hand quilted.*

The most popular appliquéd patterns, including Princess Feather, Coxcomb and Currants, Whig Rose, Rose of Sharon, and Lily, appear again and again in quilts from many different parts of the country. But quilt historians have never been able to locate any printed patterns for appliqué that were made during the mid-nineteenth century. No one has been able to figure out how quiltmakers transferred their patterns, but the fact that these patterns appear throughout the country is proof that there must have been an extensive, albeit informal, network of quiltmakers.

Quilts and the Civil War

Women on both sides of the conflict found their domestic lives radically changed by the Civil War. With blankets in short supply, women in the North collected thousands of quilts to keep soldiers warm. In the South families also gave quilts to the soldiers. But because the Union navy had blockaded Confederate ports, cutting off trade, little if any fabric got through, and some women began to weave cloth, taking up looms set aside long ago by their ancestors or learning to weave on the looms used by their slaves. The rough linsey they made has a cotton warp and a wool weft. This kind of cloth is easy to make, and even during the war, the South produced ample supplies of cotton and wool, but linsey clothing is scratchy and uncomfortable. As soon as the war was over, people stopped wearing linsey and refashioned their clothing into utilitarian quilts.

In the North women organized Ladies Aid societies to help provide uniforms and bedding for the soldiers. During the war women made about 250,000 cot-size quilts, mostly from whatever fabric they had on hand. Women also made quilts to raise money for the U.S. Sanitary Commission, which coordinated the supply effort. The first Sanitary Commission fair was organized by Mary Livermore and Jane Hoge in Chicago in the fall of 1863. The Chicago women raised $78,000, and following their example, women in other cities also held fairs at which they sold fine needlework. The quilts that were auctioned at these fairs were often returned by the highest bidder so that they could be auctioned again. The largest fair, held in New York City, raised $1,200,000, and the total amount raised by Sanitary Commission fairs was an amazing $4,500,000.

In the South women mounted similar efforts to clothe and tend to the soldiers. In 1862 several newspaper editors began a campaign to raise money for gunboats. Money was contributed in small donations, and all kinds of objects were donated to the cause. In the *Alabama Beacon* of April 11, 1862, J.J. Hutchinsons extolled the efforts of Mrs. Hatter whose beautiful silk quilt was "bid off for a sum of one hundred dollars. [The] money was immediately contributed by the persons present, and the quilt replaced in my hands to be resold for the same patriotic object." Mrs. Hatter offered still another quilt to be auctioned. Both quilts were repeatedly auctioned off, raising as much as $500. More than $4,000 was raised in Alabama, but a gunboat cost $80,000 and the newspapers called off the project.

Quiltmaker unknown, Linsey Quilt, circa 1850; 63½ by 79 inches; wool; hand pieced and hand quilted.

Mary Evans, Baltimore Album Quilt, *1852; 109 by 105 inches; cotton; hand appliquéd. Collection of the Museum of American Folk Art, New York.*

In Tennessee Mary High Prince, who was known to be a spy for the Confederacy, raised money for her cause by asking friends and family members to donate a signed quilt block in a pieced basket design she provided. Each person also paid a small amount of money. Mary Prince pieced the squares together and donated the money to the Confederacy. This kind of signed quilt is called an Album quilt; it became popular again later in the nineteenth century when young women enjoyed collecting autographs from their friends, family, teachers, and boyfriends. Some women used signature stamps and metal stencils to transfer names in indelible ink to a quilt block, but others simply wrote their names freehand with ink or embroidered their names. Quilt blocks with a white space in the center became known as Album blocks. If a family was moving away, their friends would often give them signed Album blocks with inked expressions of love and remembrance.

The most exuberant examples of this kind of quilt are Baltimore Album quilts, made in the mid-nineteenth century. These quilts were appliquéd with traditional as well as one-of-a-kind patterns. Floral sprays in baskets and floral wreaths fill the blocks, but the quilts often include images of open books, buildings, animals, and people as well.

Quilts After the Civil War

Following the Civil War, textile mills retooled quickly and began to produce badly needed cloth for the domestic market. In the 1870s a revival of interest in piecing quilts got underway as a wide variety of printed calico became available and many women purchased their first sewing machines. During this resurgence of quiltmaking, women began using shortcuts to speed up their quiltmaking; fan quilting and straight-line quilting that took as few as five or six stitches per inch replaced more elaborate antebellum quilting styles that had taken as many as 12 stitches per inch.

Coinciding with this resurgence of interest in quiltmaking, the United States Postal Service established Rural Free Delivery, putting even the most remote farm in touch with national fashions and trends. Women's magazines printed in the United States began to feature quilt patterns. The expanded postal service also made accessible fabric and quilting tools sold through mail-order catalogs.

State fairs gave quilters an opportunity to exchange patterns. Many states held their first annual fairs prior to the Civil War but suspended them during the war. In the late 1860s, fairs reopened, and in the women's buildings, often called floral halls, quiltmakers could see each other's work and sketch patterns to take home and duplicate. In 1876 a national fair was organized in Philadelphia to celebrate the centennial of the Declaration of Independence. Visitors to the fair were especially interested in the Japanese pavilion and British needlework displays. These interests spawned one of the most intense quiltmaking fads the United States has ever known—the Crazy Quilt. Made of odd-shaped pieces of silk and velvet and embellished with embroidered

Timexenia M. Morris Roper, Bursting Star, *circa 1865; 84 by 82½ inches; cotton, hand pieced and hand quilted.*

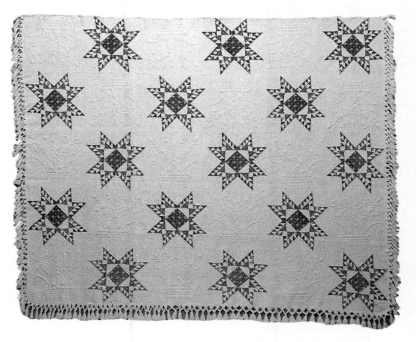

Victoria Darwin Caldwell, Feathered Star, *1865; 85¾ by 68 inches; cotton; hand pieced and hand quilted.*

Mary Mittie Belle Agner Barrier, Barnyard Quilt,
*71 by 80 inches; 1920; wool; hand pieced and
hand embroidered.*

birds, flowers, and stars, these quilts were never intended to be utilitarian bed covers. Their purpose was to show off a quilter's needlework skills. Quilters were extremely creative in acquiring the odd-shaped bits of cloth they used in their quilts. Some swapped scraps with friends or pen pals; others cut up their husbands' ties, and at least one woman passed herself off as a commercial fabric buyer and collected swatches from textile companies.

The Crazy Quilt craze continued until about 1920, but around the turn of the century, women seem to have lost interest in quilting. Few references to quiltmaking appear in women's magazines between 1900 and 1920. The fair in Knoxville, Tennessee, in 1926 listed only one quilt category; in the late 1800s a woman might enter her quilt in one of several categories.

Quilts Make a Comeback

Quiltmaking began to revive during World War I when women once again organized to raise money for a war effort. *Modern Priscilla* magazine published an article in 1917 about making a quilt to raise money for the American Red Cross. In Morristown, Tennessee, the Ladies Reading Circle asked people to make donations to support a railroad canteen for traveling soldiers. For a minimum donation, they typed the donor's name in red ink on a muslin square. For a larger donation, they wrote the name prominently in the central area of the quilt, which included a large red cross. They raised several hundred dollars. Quilts in this same *Modern Priscilla* design were also made in many other cities and towns.

Between the turn of the century and the 1920s, women who lived in cities had pretty much stopped making quilts, although quiltmaking continued in rural areas. Then suddenly, quilt exhibits and articles about antique quilts began to appear. In 1915 Marie Webster wrote the book that may have started it all, *Quilts: Their Story and How to Make Them*, which is based in part on articles about her quilts in *Ladies' Home Journal*. After people read the book, they wanted the quilt patterns, so the author set up her own mail-order pattern company. Other professional quilt designers soon followed her lead. In 1920 Anne Orr, who was internationally known for her counted cross stitch, knitting, and filet crochet patterns, began writing monthly needlework articles for *Good Housekeeping* magazine. She also set up a mail-order pattern company in her home, where she employed other needlewomen to work up samples so that her patterns would be free of errors and made with colors that harmonized with each other. Like other quilt designers, she updated traditional patterns, but her best-known quilts were based on counted cross-stitch techniques and used hundreds of one-inch squares of color.

Anne Orr, Marie Webster, and other quilt designers, including Rose Kretsinger and Mary McIlwaine, were trained artists and interior decorators, and they designed their quilts to complement the Early American furnishings that had become popular.

Letha Moore and her daughters, Step Around the Mountain, *1930; 76 by 70 inches; cotton; hand pieced and hand quilted.*

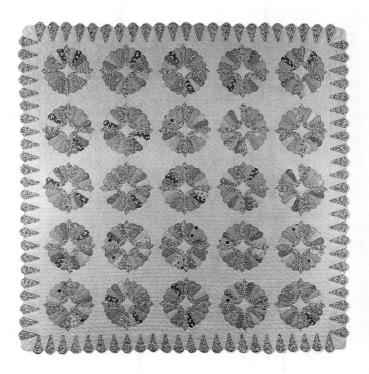

Viola Sanders Webb, Dresden Plate, *1935; 89 by 89 inches; cotton; hand pieced and hand quilted.*

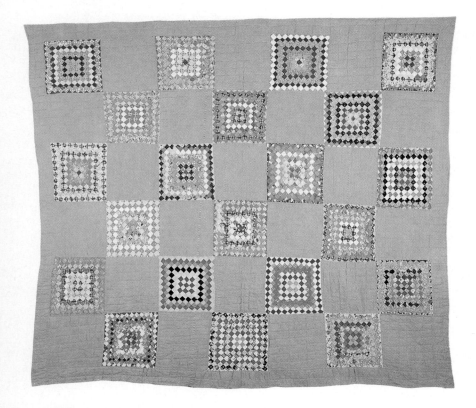

Bernice Schultz Mackey, Trip Around the World, *1927; 78½ by 71 inches; cotton; hand pieced and hand quilted.*

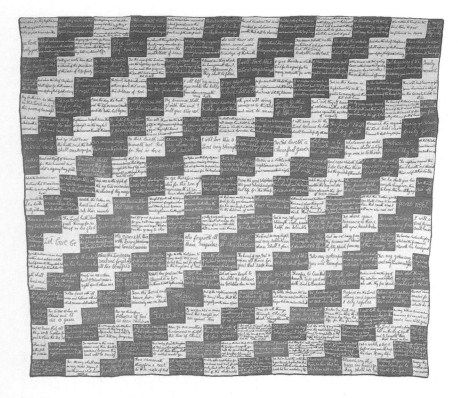

Jemima Patton Clark, Bible Verse Quilt, *1922; 85½ by 74½ inches; cotton; hand pieced, embroidered, and hand quilted.*

They revived the Medallion quilt because it was appropriate for colonial-revival beds. But they favored modern light-colored fabric and often added nontraditional scalloped edging. In the late 1920s, newspapers began to print nationally syndicated quilt columns, such as *Nancy Page's Quilt Club,* and Laura Wheeler's quilt patterns. Some newspapers hired artists to design quilt patterns that could be sold to other newspapers.

During the Great Depression, quiltmaking flourished. Colorfully printed cotton fabric was inexpensive, but some women had so little cash they had to barter for cloth or use worn-out clothing or cotton sacks. Ironically, the hard times meant there was less work in the fields and factories, and more time for leisure activities such as quilting. As the number of quilters increased, department stores and mail-order companies began to offer an array of gadgets to make quilting easier. Hot-iron transfer patterns enabled quilters to transfer piecing patterns and appliqué designs onto cloth, and eliminated the time-consuming steps of making templates and tracing around them on fabric hundreds of times. Some pre-stamped quilt tops were available. For as little as $9.00, Anne Orr offered materials for quilt tops that were stamped and ready to cut out and appliqué. Other suppliers sold quilt kits, containing precut and presorted pieces.

To save time in the quilting process, the quilter could use stamping paste with stencils. The paste cost 25 cents a box in 1934 through the Sears, Roebuck catalog and came in dark colors for stamping on light cloth and light colors for stamping on dark cloth. According to the catalog, the paste would not smear like a pencil line, but it could not easily be removed. Stencils cost 25 cents each. They were made of tough transparent paper and perforated with such traditional quilting designs as wreaths, cables, pineapples, and vines. To use stamping paste and a stencil, the quilter wet a cotton ball with benzine, rubbed it over the cake of stamping paste, and then stroked it lightly over the perforations in a stencil positioned on the quilt top. When the stencil was removed, lines of tiny dots showed the quilter where to place the quilting stitches.

Someone on the staff of Sears, Roebuck and Company was probably thinking about the thousands of yards of fabric and all the quilting gadgets the company would sell when he proposed a national quilt exhibit for the World's Fair in Chicago. The contest was announced in the Sears, Roebuck catalog in January 1933, just four months before the deadline on May 15. From the nearly 25,000 quilts that were submitted, 30 were chosen to hang at the Sears Building in Chicago. Four judges, including quilt designers Anne Orr and Mary McIlwaine, reviewed the top 30 quilts and chose one submitted by Margaret Caden of Lexington, Kentucky, as the grand-prize winner. She won $1000 and the honor of having her quilt given to First Lady Eleanor Roosevelt. Sears also published her pattern, renaming it Bluegrass Star.

Quilt exhibits again became popular attractions at state and county fairs. At some fairs so many quilts of certain patterns were submitted that quilts were often exhibited and judged with other quilts of the same pattern. At several Ohio fairs, there were competitions exclusively for Double Wedding Ring, Dresden Plate and Grandmother's Flower Garden quilts. Exhibits of antique quilts were also popular during the 1930s.

As World War II swept around the globe, the American textile industry began to produce materials for the war effort. Soon after the United States entered the war, fabric for home use was once again in short supply, but this time women did not take out their looms and produce cloth, or make quilts for soldiers or to raise money. Instead, many women went to work in factories producing equipment, guns, ammunition, and airplanes.

When World War II was over, advertisers targeted women for new products. They enticed women with time-saving appliances, hoping they would leave their jobs, return home, and raise families in new suburban homes. Looking back into history for long-lost values and traditions was discouraged, and quiltmaking all but disappeared during the 1950s and 1960s. Women in rural areas continued to make quilts as they always had, but new quiltmakers were no longer encouraged through magazine and newspaper articles.

An informal network of quiltmakers and quilt researchers developed to try to keep quiltmaking alive. Mimeographed newsletters such as *The Quilt News and Hobbies* printed in Jameson, Missouri, by Georgia Williams provided patterns, quilting tips, and the addresses of other quiltmakers. Barbara Bannister sold needlework and quilt patterns from her home in Michigan. She encouraged the reissue of Ruby Short McKim's 1930s book *One Hundred and One Patchwork Patterns*. But these women were ahead of their time.

Quilts Today

Jonathan Holstein and Gail Van der Hoof get the credit for starting the second quilt revival of the twentieth century. In 1971 they organized an exhibit entitled "Abstract Design in American Quilts" for the Whitney Museum of American Art in New York. Other museums had organized similar quilt exhibits, such as the "Optical Quilts" exhibit at the Newark Museum in 1965, but none of these shows received as much attention as the show at the Whitney. Suddenly, the art world took notice; quilts had moved from the bed to the gallery wall. Artists began to experiment with fabric, creating innovative fashions and sculpture as well as wall pieces. They often turned to antique quilts to gain inspiration from their designs, color harmonies, intricate stitching patterns, and inventiveness.

The current quilt revival reflects earlier quilt revivals when designers sought out traditional patterns and updated them using new fabrics, gadgets, and design elements. But this quilt revival is broader than earlier quilt revivals. It encompasses quilt history, the preservation of quilts, traditional quiltmaking, art quilts, and quilted clothing, and after more than twenty years, it continues to gain momentum.

Sarah Moore, Schoolhouse, *circa 1920; 79¹/₂ by 84¹/₂ inches; cotton; hand pieced and hand tied.*

Lillian Jackson Jones, The World's Fair Quilt, *circa 1924; 75¹/₂ by 95¹/₂ inches; cotton; hand pieced and hand quilted.*

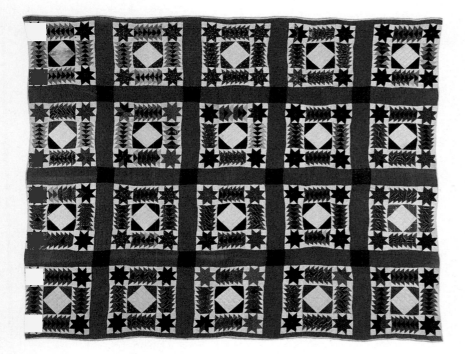

Mary Haynes, Patriotic quilt of unnamed design, circa 1890; 83 by 63 inches; cotton; hand pieced and hand quilted. Many quilts made at the time of the bicentennial echo the design of this quilt.

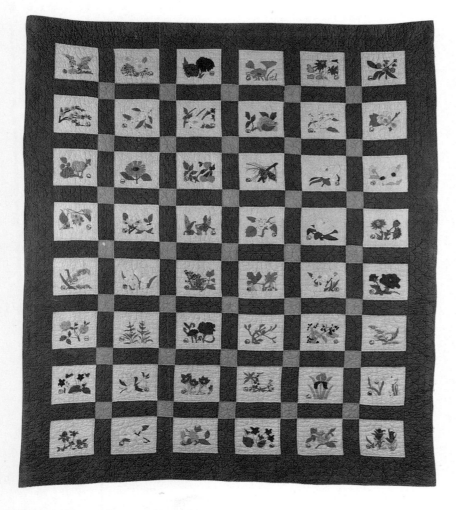

Rubye Nelson Seymour, State Flower Quilt, 1933; 61 by 77 inches; cotton; hand pieced and hand quilted.

The 1976 celebration of the nation's bicentennial fueled patriotic fervor and an interest in the country's past. Quiltmaking became an accessible symbol of colonial domestic life, and hundreds of quilts were made from red, white, and blue fabric. The centennial of the Statue of Liberty and bicentennial of the U.S. Constitution were also celebrated with quilt contests, traveling exhibits, and community-made album quilts.

In many parts of the country, people have contributed blocks to make quilts that commemorate anniversaries, events, and causes that are important to their communities, and two enormous nationwide quilt projects have brought people together to express their common concerns. The Peace Ribbon was made up of thousands of panels that graphically demonstrated their creators' hopes for a world without war. The AIDS Memorial Quilt now also contains thousands of panels, each of which is a memorial to a person who has died of AIDS, made by his or her friends and family.

Today, 20 quilt magazines are in regular publication, including *Quilter's Newsletter Magazine*, which was started in 1969 by Bonnie Lehan, *Ladies' Circle Patchwork Quilt*, and *Quilter's Journal*. These publications have taken over the role of printing quilt patterns and offering advice to quilters that women's magazines and newspapers had in the past. These quilt magazines have had an immense impact on the current revival, which might have died out had it not been for the success of quilt magazines. Quilt books published since the early 1970s far outnumber the quilt books written from the 1930s through the 1960s. How-to books, historical accounts of quiltmaking, and calendars have also fueled interest in quiltmaking and quilt collecting.

Quilt guilds have now replaced old-fashioned quilting bees. Guilds vary in size; some meet weekly, others only occasionally; but basically the members meet to quilt together and to learn from each other. Most guilds organize annual quilt exhibits and provide demonstrations of quiltmaking to school groups and community fairs. They also carry on the tradition of quilting to provide support for charitable causes. Many quilt groups make quilts for sick children. Some groups make quilts to raffle or auction off to raise money for worthy causes. The National Quilting Association, founded in 1970, serves as an umbrella for many quilt guilds, publishing a quarterly magazine called *Patchwork Patter*, organizing an annual quilt exhibit and conference, and providing judge and teacher certification programs.

Quilt National provides an opportunity for the artists who are redefining the quilt to exhibit their designs. The juried show is held every other year in Athens, Ohio. The quilts in the show then travel for two years, and the exhibit's catalog further disseminates information about these innovative quilts. Even though Quilt National always generates heated discussion among quilters and other artists, the show is a rich source of inspiration for today's quiltmakers.

AIDS Memorial Quilt, *Washington, D.C., 1988.*

Martha Secords, Lone Star, *circa 1870; 101 by 101 inches; cotton; hand pieced and hand quilted.*

In 1980 a group of women in Kentucky embarked on an ambitious project to record historical and technical data on quilts made in that state before 1900. After documenting a wide variety of quilts, they chose a group of representative quilts for a traveling exhibit and wrote an accompanying catalog. The exhibit was so well received that similar projects in other states soon followed. Currently, there are at least 53 quilt projects underway or recently completed. One benefit of these surveys is that thousands of quilts have been brought out for viewing and analysis. Photographs of them and their histories will now be preserved. The project organizers have also taken advantage of the opportunity to provide the owners of antique quilts with information on their proper care.

There are now two museums devoted to quilt history: the American Museum of Quilts and Related Arts in San Jose, California, and the New England Museum of Quilts in Lowell, Massachusetts. Other major museums have large quilt collections. These include the Art Institute of Chicago, the Smithsonian Institution in Washington, D.C., and the Los Angeles Museum of Art. Urban museums and smaller regional museums regularly mount quilt exhibits, and some of these exhibits have traveled throughout the country and around the world. Museum shows often trigger interest in a certain kind of quilt. Amish quilts, African-American quilts, and more recently, Depression Era quilts have become especially popular in turn, inspiring quiltmakers and increasing their value as collectibles.

Since colonial times, quilts have been in our homes, warming us, comforting our children, giving us joy as we make and share them, and helping us remember our mothers, grandmothers, and great-grandmothers. They have witnessed the good times and bad times for our families and our country. Quilts are the pieced records not only of the clothes we were wearing, the kinds of fabrics we liked, and our favorite colors, but also of our values and our dreams. Today, quilts are as much a part of American life as ever, whether they are on a frame in the process of being quilted, tucked away safely in a closet, hanging proudly on a living room wall, or keeping us warm at night.

Mrs. D.P. Walker, Crown of Thorns, *circa 1840; 74³/₄ by 87¹/₄ inches; cotton; hand pieced and hand quilted.*

Quiltmaker unknown, Log Cabin, *circa 1880; 67 by 62 inches; silk; hand pieced.*

Jane A. Sassaman, Light Study; *36 by 36 inches; all-cotton; machine pieced and machine quilted.*

Amish Country Collection, Jacob's Ladder; *45 by 45 inches; cotton blends; machine pieced and hand quilted.*

Michael A. Cummings, Haitian Boat People III; *96 by 60 inches; cotton and cotton blends; machine pieced and machine quilted.*

AMERICA'S BEST QUILTERS

Today's American quiltmakers are creating an astounding variety of truly remarkable quilts. Some skilled quilters craft exquisite traditional quilts for beds and baby cribs; others concentrate on elaborate wall pieces that blend needlework with other media or use traditional techniques to make distinctively personal statements. In the following pages you will meet 75 of America's best quilters and quilting collectives. Even though the quilts they produce are as varied as the quiltmakers themselves, you will find that they all share a commitment to carrying on the tradition of quiltmaking.

Quiltmaking in the best American tradition has always been experimental. The history of America's quilts is a record of successful attempts to expand the definition of this medium, with each new trend adding to the extensive vocabulary of quilting techniques and quilt designs. If you think that some of today's art quilts have taken quiltmaking too far away from its roots, imagine how strange the first Crazy Quilts must have seemed a hundred years ago to people who had been used to seeing calico patchwork quilts. Diversity and experimentation that blends the old with the new are hallmarks of the best American quiltmaking. Many of the quilts in this book include the same elements that were first used to make nineteenth century Crazy Quilts—beads, metallic threads, bright silk, photographs, paintings, and found objects, while others incorporate or reinterpret patterns and techniques that date back to colonial times.

The quiltmakers in this book are all incredibly skilled at their craft. But each quilter is unique in the way in which she or he uses the techniques of quiltmaking. Many quilters explore the traditional themes of geometric patterns and flowers; others make quilts, using fabric or mixed media, that interpret new themes, such as architecture, humor, or personal imagery. All of these quilters experiment with color and pattern, using cotton, cotton-blend, silk, and synthetic fabrics and threads. Many paint or dye the fabric they use in their quilts; some use antique or handmade fabrics. Several quilters use only fabric scraps they have on hand. Traditional quilts are neatly finished, but many art quilters include loose threads and rough edges in their work. The standard rectangular format of traditional quilts inspires some quilters to find unique ways to organize patterns and images within its prescribed shape, but other quilters are challenged to make quilts in new shapes and sizes, to make two-sided quilts, or to break out of the rectangle in other dynamic ways.

Many quiltmakers in this book are self-taught quilters whose formal training may have been in mathematics, science, nursing, teaching, or the fine arts. Some of today's best quiltmakers learned their craft from their mothers or grandmothers; others joined guilds or took classes and workshops. Many have been sewing since they were children, and almost every quilter shares a lifelong love of fabric. Many quiltmakers made their first quilt because they wanted to make a special gift for someone they loved. But several quiltmakers who had been working in other media turned to quiltmaking when their children were little, because an unfinished quilt can be worked on at odd moments when children are sleeping or playing.

The beautiful quilts in this book encompass the vast range of quilts that are being made today. As you enjoy them and read about the quiltmakers who made them, remember that quilts have always been much more than utilitarian bed covers. Quilts traditionally have significance. They are made to celebrate the most important events in our lives—a marriage, the birth of a child, or an important friendship. A family that is given an album quilt to take with them when they move to another community will always cherish the fond memories of the friends who made the quilt. Every scrap quilt is filled with memories called to mind by a snippet of dad's tie, a piece of the baby's dress, and a swatch of sister's petticoat. During the slow meditative process of piecing, appliquéing, and quilting, the quiltmaker often ascribes meaning to the quilt's patterns and colors. A quilt is a personal and artistic expression of the quiltmaker. It may be abstract, geometric, or a collection of recognizable images, but a quilt will always tell us something important about the quilter who made it.

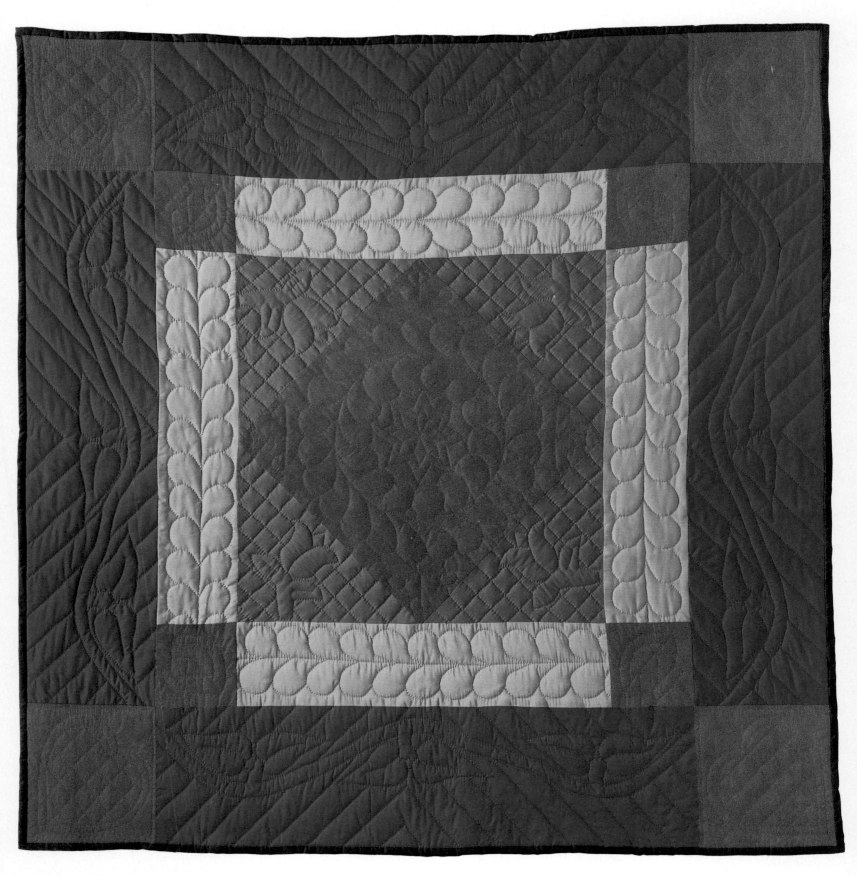

Amish Center Diamond; *45 by 45 inches; cotton blends; machine pieced and hand quilted.*

AMISH COUNTRY COLLECTION

Beautiful bold colors and superb stitching are the hallmarks of the quilts in the Amish Country Collection that are the wonderful handiwork of Amish and Mennonite women. Deanna Wish, who owns the Amish Country Collection, became interested in quilts when an Amish woman suggested that she include quilts in her collection.

The quilts from the Amish Country Collection are made according to traditional methods and techniques. Deanna says that the Amish and Mennonite craftspeople with whom she works still live lives based on their historical values and traditions. Many do not have telephones, and few have electricity. Women still use foot-powered treadle machines for sewing. Agriculture remains their primary work, so production schedules for quilts and other items in the Amish Country Collection vary with the seasons and the activities of the community. ''These are a very independent people,'' Deanna says, ''and they work within their own time frame.'' Once she visited an Amish family on January 15, only to find that a major family celebration was in progress. It turned out that the family was celebrating Christmas because everyone had been too busy to do so on December 25.

Amish and Mennonite quiltmakers learn their craft from other members of their families, and sewing skills are passed on from mother to daughter. Quiltmakers use sewing machines for piecing, but they quilt by hand, frequently in the beautiful flower, feather, and cable patterns for which this group is well known. Although many Amish Country Collection quilts have traditional designs, such as Broken Star and Bars, quilts made for the English, as Amish people call anyone who is not Amish, may have nontraditional elements. An Amish quilter would be unlikely to make an appliquéd quilt for her own family, and she would never use print fabric. But these restrictions are relaxed for quilts in the collection, and quilters use both appliqué and print fabrics.

Deanna says that she gets a lot of requests for particular color combinations and special designs from the interior designers and architects with whom she often works. Color is a main concern, she says, and many quilts in her collection combine contemporary color preferences with old designs. Deanna supplies a quilter with the fabric and a design. It is up to her to execute the design and add her own stitching pattern.

Between 70 and 90 quilters make quilts for the Amish Country Collection. They make as many as 1,500 quilts a year. Some quilts are made by several members of a family or by a group of friends, since for Amish women quilting is a social activity as well as a way to supplement their incomes. Because of the skill of all the quilters and the evenness of their stitches, it is impossible to determine whether one of these lovely quilts was made by one pair of hands or many.

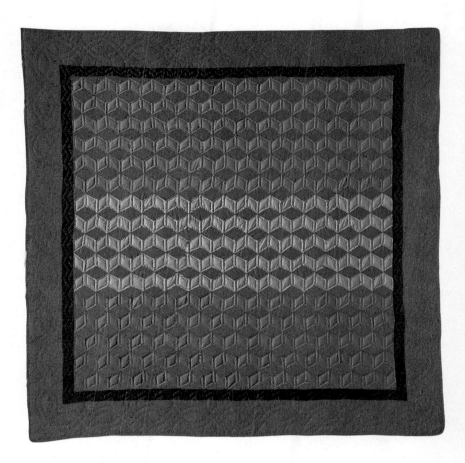

Tumbling Block; *65 by 55 inches; cotton blends; machine pieced and hand quilted.*

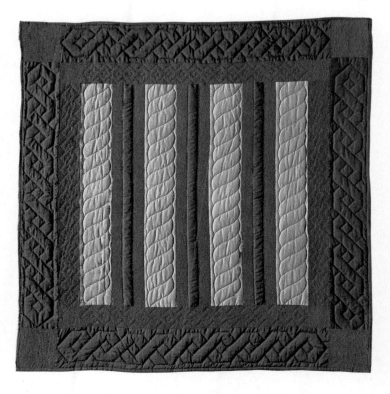

Bar Quilt; *45 by 46 inches; cotton blends; machine pieced and hand quilted.*

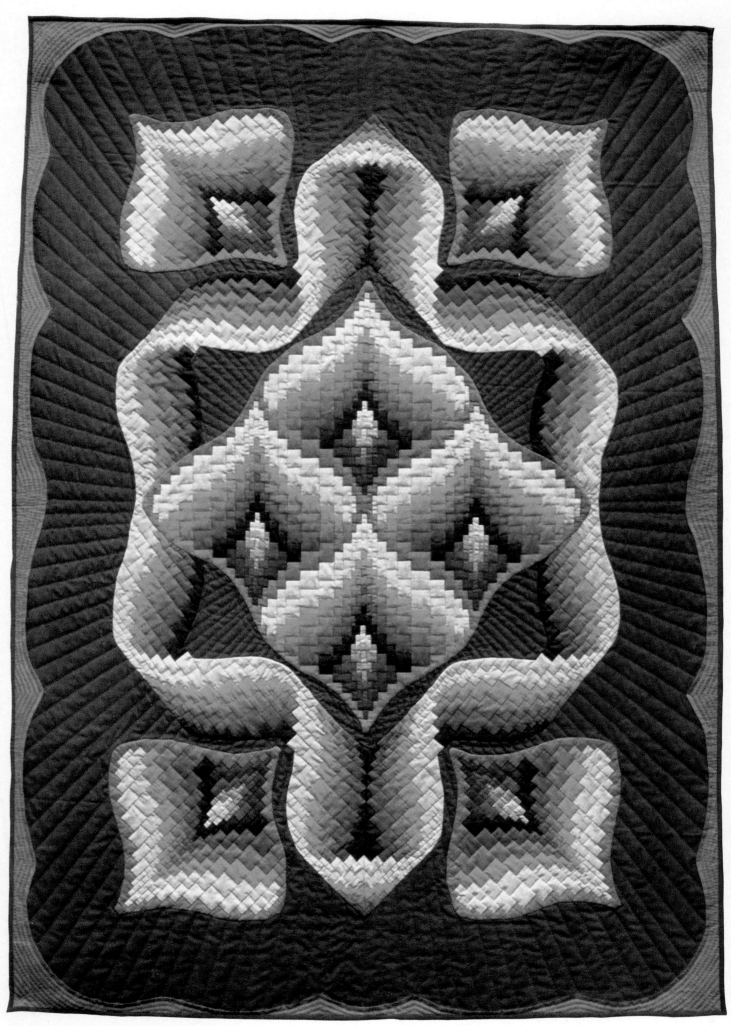

Peacock Puzzle: Variations on a Seam; *36¹/₂ by
51¹/₂ inches; all-cotton; machine pieced,
appliquéd, and machine and hand quilted.*

JENNIFER AMOR

After breaking package after package of needles, Jennifer Amor gave up on her first quilt, a brightly colored Drunkard's Path for which she attempted to use two double-loft batts. But it was not long until this self-taught quilter successfully completed another quilt and began a new career as a fiber artist. Before becoming a professional quilter, Jennifer had designed boutique clothing and worked as a journalist.

In her work Jennifer uses both machine and hand piecing and quilting, appliqué, and other traditional techniques. She also uses such nontraditional methods as fabric painting to create her highly original quilts. Her work includes pieced quilts that look like Bargello needlepoint, graphed floral designs, pictorial quilts, and abstract patterns. Bargello designs inspired Jennifer to make *Peacock Puzzle: Variations on a Seam* and *Moroccan Mosaic*, using an original technique she developed especially for these quilts. Working from a graph, she created sets of fabric strips that she sewed together to form a loose design. Jennifer then hand appliquéd the strips to the background and finished the quilt with a combination of machine and hand quilting. Because she wanted the central motif in *Peacock Puzzle* to appear to float, the quilting lines radiate from the center outward, creating a stunning three-dimensional effect.

Moroccan Mosaic was actually the first Bargello quilt. It was inspired by a trip to Morocco, where the vivid colors of the Bay of Tangiers and the intricate mosaics on mosques intrigued the artist. Originally, the piece was entirely hand quilted, but the stitches were uneven because of the thickness of the seams. Jennifer recently pulled out the quilting stitches from the center portion of the quilt and requilted it by machine so that it now hangs better. The artist left the borders hand quilted in the Ogee pattern to reflect the piece's Moroccan influence.

The Kool-Aid® Quilt—Charlotte's Web is the delightful outcome of a project Jennifer designed to teach children about quilts as a part of the South Carolina Arts Commission artists-in-education program, which places working artists in schools. During her residency, Jennifer has the children dye fabrics in Kool-Aid® and use fabric crayons and paints to design quilt blocks, which the children sew together by hand. The blocks are usually based on a theme, and the one for this quilt is the popular children's book *Charlotte's Web*. A handprint border includes each child's handprint and autograph. Jennifer completes the quilt with sashing, batting, a back, and machine quilting, and returns it to the school so that the children have a lasting reminder of their experience. During a school year, Jennifer can do residencies in as many as 22 schools. "All my kids successfully complete a school quilt," she says, "and often it's those children who have the least academic success who make the best sewers and artists."

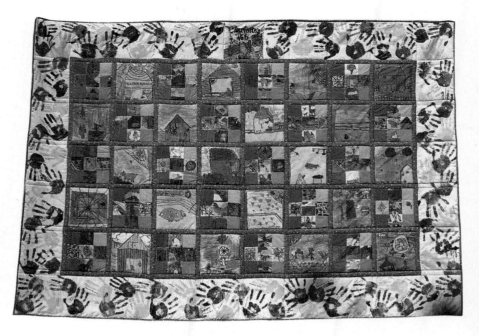

The Kool-Aid® Quilt—Charlotte's Web; *82 by 57 inches; cotton and cotton blends; machine and hand pieced, and machine quilted. Made by the third-grade classes of Nursery Road Elementary School, Irmo, South Carolina.*

Moroccan Mosaic; *42 by 42 inches; cotton and cotton blends; machine pieced and machine and hand quilted.*

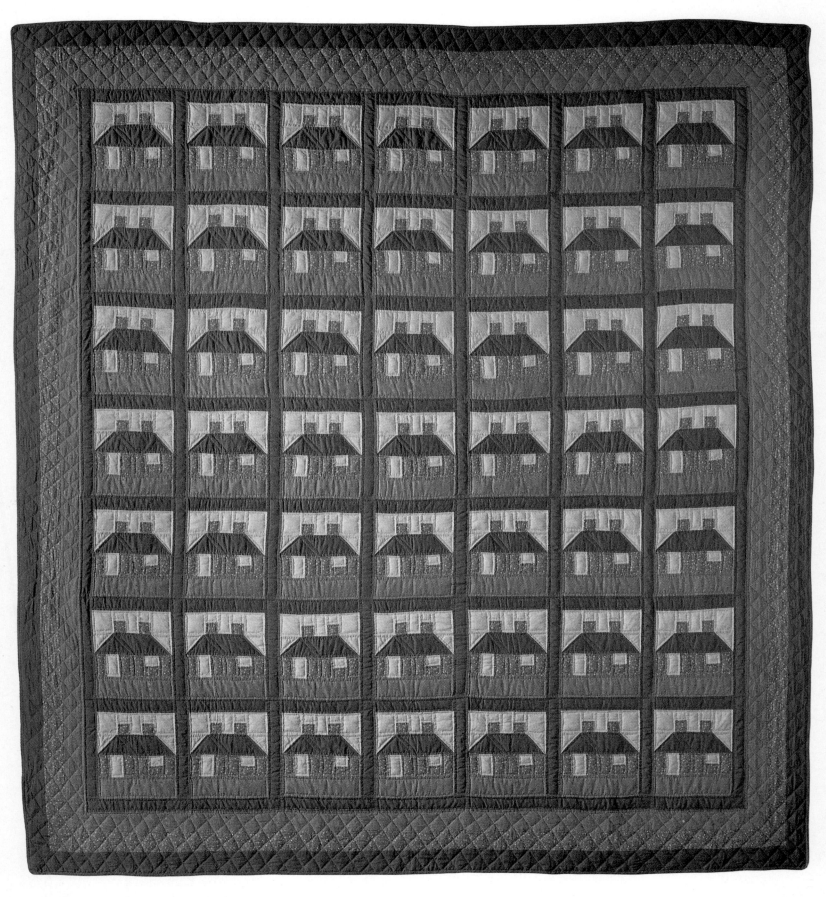

School House; *93 by 106 inches; cotton blends;
machine pieced and hand quilted.*

APPALACHIAN FIRESIDE CRAFTS

Appalachian Fireside Crafts makes exquisite, highly valued quilts with meticulous attention to detail. Over the last 25 years, the group has grown from a few people looking for ways to supplement their incomes to a highly successful, self-sufficient organization of more than 400 people with their own showcase outlet, the Appalachian Fireside Gallery.

Jerry Workman, one founder of the group, recalls working with the Office of Economic Opportunity during the 1960s when there were many people in the rural areas of Kentucky who wanted to work but could not get jobs. Women were especially hard-pressed because they needed work that could be done at home without neglecting their chores or seasonal agricultural work. Particularly, they needed something that they could do during the long mountain winters. Jerry had the idea that they should revive the indigenous handicrafts of the area, and the idea of Appalachian Fireside Crafts was born. At first, five craftspeople made pinecone wreaths, but with funding from Save the Children, the group established a three-pronged program that covers training in techniques and design, production, and marketing. Within a few years, their list of products has expanded to include quilts, rag rugs, hand weavings, furniture, corn shuck dolls, baskets, and decorative wooden objects.

Between 30 and 65 quilters work for the group at any one time. They use traditional patterns that have long been popular in Kentucky, including Dresden Plate, Log Cabin, School House, and Lone Star. The quilters have free rein in their choice of designs, but Lone Star and a local innovation called Dollie's Star, which uses appliqué rather than traditional piecing, are the favorites of both the quilters and the customers.

Most quilts are made by three women. The piecer picks the pattern, buys fabric from the group's well-stocked warehouse, cuts pieces, and sews them together to make the top. Then the quilter takes over. She uses the stitching design she thinks works best with the pattern of the quilt top. When the quilting is complete, a binder finishes off the quilt.

The quilting itself is done two ways: quilting by the piece (stitching that follows the block pattern of a quilt) or free form (elaborate patterns of stitches on quilts with large plain areas). The Appalachian Fireside quilters use needles rather than pencils to mark their quilting lines. They spread the quilt top on the floor or on a table, and mark off the design by dragging a needle backward over the surface to indicate the lines the stitching should follow.

In 1976 the American Museum in Bath, England, honored the group by designating their work as the best quilts in the United States. Since 1970, when the group started numbering their pieces, they have made about six thousand quilts.

School House/Log Cabin: *98 by 113 inches; cotton blends; machine pieced, hand appliquéd, and hand quilted.*

Log Cabin; *92 by 106 inches; cotton blends; machine pieced and hand quilted.*

APPALACHIAN FIRESIDE CRAFTS

Winding Ways; *98 by 113 inches; cotton blends;*
machine pieced and hand quilted.

Dresden Plate; *82 by 100 inches; cotton blends; machine pieced, hand appliquéd, and hand quilted.*

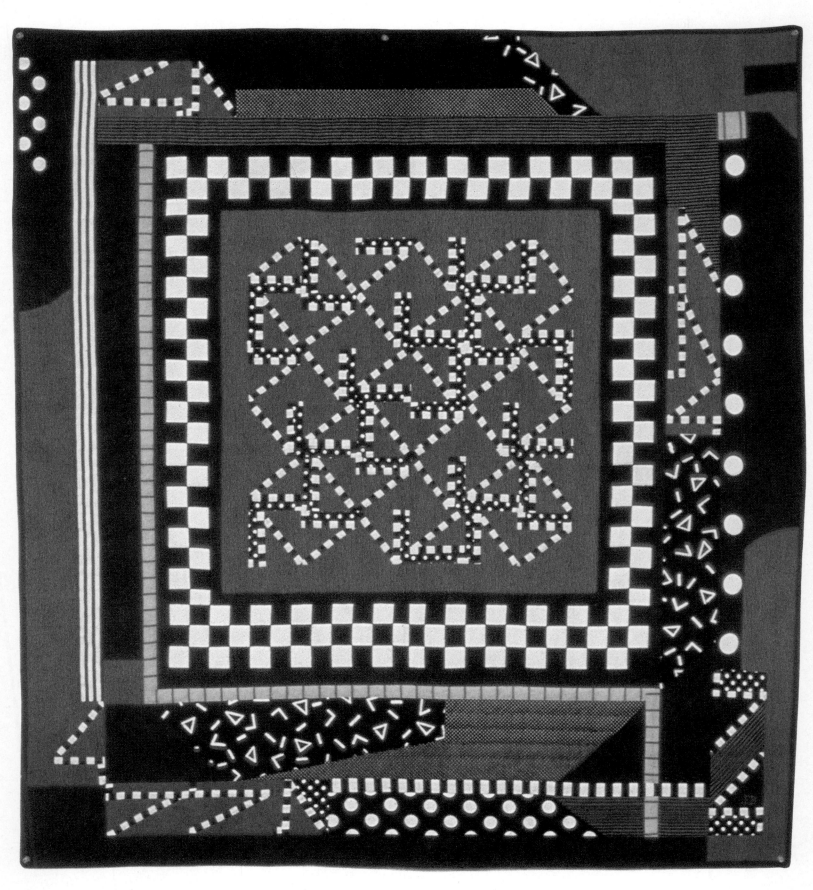

African Rhythms; *55 by 59 inches; cotton and
rayon; machine pieced and hand quilted.*

JUDY BECKER

While her children were young, Judy Becker found that quilting gave her a way to explore color and design that wasn't too messy and could be done in the short stretches of time her busy schedule left free. She taught herself to quilt, starting with an Ohio Star bed quilt and using Beth Gutcheon's *The Perfect Patchwork Primer* as her bible of technique. "I'm still grateful to that book for my start," she says. Judy has now made about a hundred quilts, many based on original designs inspired by music, travel, familiar scenes, and the work of her favorite artist, Matisse.

Butterfly Baroque presents stark color combinations and a striking graphic design. Even though some of the quilt blocks repeat, they vary in size and seem to dissolve and scatter into the background fabric as they move out from the center of the quilt. The background fabric is a print of moths and served as the inspiration for the quilt; Judy says that she is loathe to look for symbolism in her work, but there are certain comparisons to be made between the balance of strength and fragility in both moths and quilts.

The artist often listens to jazz while she hand quilts, and music inspired *African Rhythms*, one in a four-quilt series she calls the Modern Jazz Quartet. The red fabric provides the sense of "heat" that an African beat demands, and the touch of brilliant orange is an unexpected counterpoint. Judy designed the sparkling center of the quilt before she started to sew, but the rest of the piece grew border by border in an improvisational manner. "Since the inspiration was jazz, that somehow seems appropriate," says the artist. She was so taken by the improvisation that she finished the quilt in one month.

Hockney's Runes has a subdued ground, but it gets a brilliant lift from the deep-red lines that crisscross the surface. Judy's inspiration for this quilt came from a photo collage of a garden in Kyoto, Japan, by artist David Hockney. The center of the quilt represents the peaceful and serene central courtyard of the garden; the lines are the paths that wander through the grounds, some of them leading to the garden walls. The random shapes on the left that are set against a white ground suggest footprints left by visitors to the garden. The work also recalls the mazes found in many elegant walled gardens in Europe.

Judy carefully schedules time to work into her week, at least three or four hours a day, seven days a week. "It is like any other job, not found time," she says. Family, friends, and relatives have learned to respect the seriousness of her intent and do not disrupt her scheduled hours. The striking products of this work time have appeared in juried and invitational shows throughout the United States and in Japan and Colombia, as well as in books and journals. Her work has also won many awards.

Butterfly Baroque; *61 by 57 inches; all-cotton; machine pieced, appliquéd, and machine and hand quilted.*

Hockney's Runes; *57 by 54 inches; all-cotton; machine pieced and hand quilted.*

Winter; *72 by 72 inches; cotton and cotton blends; machine pieced and hand quilted.*

SUE BENNER

Expressionist landscapes and other personal interpretations of nature are the subjects of Sue Benner's gloriously hued quilts. Sue has degrees in molecular biology and biomedical illustration, and never expected to become a quilter, even though she had made a scrap quilt for a school project when she was ten. But a class in fabric design encouraged her to look in new directions, and Sue soon found herself making a series of quilts based on biomedical themes for her honors thesis. Her first quilt for this project was a plant cell batiked on cotton, complete with chloroplasts and mitochondria. By the time she received her master's degree, she was well on the way to a quilting career.

Sue had learned basic sewing skills as a child, and her mother helped her make a few simple quilts, but she is essentially a self-taught quilter. She has now made about sixty quilts that combine her own hand-painted and hand-dyed fabrics with commercially printed ones in vivid and startling arrays of color and contrast.

The inspiration for her glowing quilt *Evening Sky* was many evenings of appreciative sky watching. The color gradations from deep blue to periwinkle represent the darkening sky, the red and rust are the earth, and the colorful appliqués that float merrily over the surface are clouds catching the disappearing sun. "I am fascinated by horizons, by the interface of land and sky," Sue says. She set the grids at angles to symbolize the forces of nature, and her simple quilting design reinforces a sense of motion.

Winter is one quilt in a series of four that were inspired by Monet's garden paintings. It is based on a Nine Patch structure, with some additional elements from Central Diamond and Sunshine and Shadow traditional designs. The central "hot" area represents a cozy hearth as well as the artist's excitement about cold weather, but Sue made the border in cool icy tones. The quilting carries out Sue's impression of the dual warm and cold aspects of winter: The center is flame quilted, and a quilting pattern of bare tree branches enhances the corners and borders. For many months this quilt was a disorganized collection of nine patches on Sue's work wall: "I had painted and gathered all these wild colors, with no idea of why they were winter to me. When the thought of fire in the central diamond came to me, the icy outer border became the obvious solution."

A World of Reasons II is part of a provocative series the artist created in response to her decision to get married. In it she used an X to represent the concepts "ex-pectation" and "ex-planation." "As I worked on this series, the shapes began to look like a sliced-up global map," Sue says, "or a whole world of reasons," which became the title. Sue dyed the silk for this quilt with a rainbow of fiber reactive dyes, using a combination of techniques that the artist has developed over the years.

Evening Sky; *48 by 36 inches; silk; machine pieced, machine appliquéd, and machine quilted.*

A World of Reasons II *(detail); 107 by 42 inches; silk; machine pieced and machine quilted.*

Peterborough: Regional Images; *60 by 60 inches;*
cyanotype prints on cotton; machine pieced and
machine quilted.

TAFI BROWN

Tafi Brown uses cyanotype photography, a method of blueprinting developed in the 1840s, in her award-winning wall quilts. The artist adapted the process which produces blueprints that do not fade, to print images on cotton cloth. "I think of it as painting with light," she says. She prints images from Kodalith negatives, which print only light and dark, on fabric treated with light-sensitive chemicals. Tafi then makes quilts using these images, which are always blue.

In addition to being a quilter, Tafi is also a free-lance photographer and designs timber-frame houses. She fell into quilting "strictly by chance," she says. Tafi had been a potter and ceramics teacher, and was working with cyanotype and other kinds of photography with the idea of printing photographs on pottery. At that time her family was building a new home, and she decided that it would be fun to document and illustrate the building process by making a blueprint quilt from the slides she had taken as the project progressed from dismantling a barn to building the house from the barn timbers. In the course of making the quilt, Tafi discovered that by piecing the cyanotypes together in different ways—upside down or reversed, for example—she could create endless varieties of patterns. More quilt ideas flowed naturally from there, and experimentation with this new craft rapidly became an obsession.

Tree Three was inspired by winter silhouettes and the intricate and beautiful patterns made by the bare branches of trees against the stark background of that season. Tafi photographed single images of trees and then used them as modules to create kaleidoscopic images of trees throughout the quilt. But if you look closely, you can identify the image that began the pattern. As in all the artist's cyanotype quilts, blue predominates, but judicious use of other colors adds flashes of energy and relieves the drama of the monochromatic images.

Peterborough: Regional Images, made as a commission for a bank, is graphically powerful and filled with captivating images. The artist concentrated on the geographic locale of the bank and its branches in her photography, as she wanted both abstract and individually recognizable images in the quilt. For Tafi design is always the most difficult part, and in this quilt she faced an additional challenge— incorporating a picture of a Saint Bernard dog, the bank's mascot.

Although house building is a theme common to many of Tafi's quilts, *McCarty/Norlander Raising* is a happy commemoration of a specific event—the raising of her friends' timber-frame house. "Their living space is small," she says, "so I designed a small quilt." Tafi took photographs as work on the house progressed, and then printed, assembled, and highlighted them with strips and blocks of solid-color and print fabrics to create a lively reminder of the excitement of house building.

Tree Three; *58 by 38½ inches; cyanotype prints on cotton; machine pieced and machine quilted.*

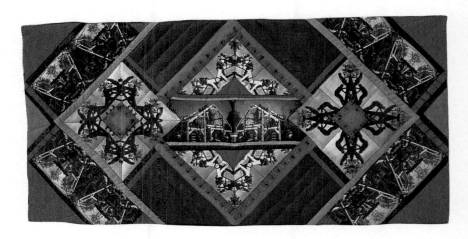

McCarty/Norlander Raising; *24 by 12 inches; cyanotype prints on cotton; machine pieced and machine quilted.*

Star and Feathers; *94 by 108 inches; all-cotton; hand quilted.*

BETTY JO BUCICH

B etty Jo Bucich makes traditional quilts, and her favorite pattern is Love Ring. "I'm not a designer," she says. But her deceptively simple whole-cloth quilts, enhanced by her exquisite stitching of complex designs, have their own unique artistry. She began quilting about ten years ago. "I needed a new hobby," Betty Jo says, "and a friend suggested quilting." After taking a class in sampler quilting, she went on to sign up for as many classes in different quilting techniques as she could find.

Even though she has made only two white-on-white whole-cloth quilts, Betty Jo feels that this is the kind of quilting she does best. *Star and Feathers*, her first whole-cloth quilt, started with her husband giving her a marked quilt top as a birthday present. Betty Jo set to work enthusiastically, even though the pattern was elaborate, with a complex central medallion, swirling Quaker feathers, deeply looped corners, and background crosshatching. The quilt demanded fastidiously tiny and close-set stitches. "It was the most intricate piece that I had done until that time," Betty Jo says. In spite of all the detail, Betty Jo found that her work went quickly: It took her about six hundred hours and a thousand yards of thread to complete this quilt. But she enjoyed every minute and every stitch, and thinks that this quilt is her best work to date.

Betty Jo's second white-on-white quilt, *Double Wedding Ring*, was an anniversary present for her daughter and son-in-law. The pattern in this quilt is almost identical to the lovely traditional one used in pieced quilts, but in Betty Jo's quilt the design is delineated through meticulous stitching rather than contrasting pieces of fabric. The overlapping rings with their pretty central floral motifs are carried out on this large quilt with delicate and even stitches that show the pattern in stunning relief. Like Betty Jo's other whole-cloth quilts, *Double Wedding Ring* was marked by an Amish woman who lives in a nearby town. The quilter uses a 14-inch hoop for her work, holding a spoon on the underside of the quilt and using a thimble on her finger as she makes her precise stitches.

Even though her white-on-white quilts are Betty Jo's favorites, her skill is obvious in her pieced quilts as well. *Love Ring* is an explosion of concentric diamonds that never seems to end. Composed of solids and prints, Betty Jo had intended this to be her first Amish quilt, but she did not find out until after her quilt was finished that Amish quilters do not use print fabrics. Her biggest challenge in this work, she says, was the curved pieces, which she had not worked with before.

Betty Jo usually works on quilting projects every day, finding that intricate work is "a good way to relax." She prefers to work at a leisurely and regular pace, but she has also been known to devote herself exclusively to quilting for whatever amount of time is necessary if she has a deadline for a quilt show coming up.

Love Ring; 70 by 86 inches; all-cotton; machine-pieced and hand quilted.

Star and Feathers *(detail)*.

Shadows in the Snow; *85 by 104 inches; all-cotton, machine pieced and hand quilted.*

CAROL E. BUTZKE

Carol E. Butzke gives her quilts a strong sense of history and tradition, but she makes them her own by including design elements that refer to events from her own life and her observations of the world around her. One of her quilts, *Shadows in the Snow*, is based on a traditional pattern known as Pine Tree or Tree of Life, but Carol has expanded the traditional design so that it recalls her family's love of skiing and the beauty of Wisconsin winters. The quilt is bordered with an unusual blue pattern of the quilter's own design. Because she likes surprises, she quilted a scene of her family skiing in the lower border on the back of the quilt that is not visible from the front. The trees as well as the family scene are quilted in blue to highlight them on the reverse side. While she was making this quilt, Carol thought that she had developed a unique quilting design for the open white areas, but she later found the same design of a snow-laden branch on an old Pine Tree quilt. "I guess everything old is new again," she says.

"I plunge into things; I've never been one to start anything small," says Carol. Her first quilt was a double-size sampler for her then-newborn son. "I figured that by the time he was ready for a large bed, the quilt would be finished." It was completed well before the baby had outgrown his crib, and Carol has gone on to make fifty more quilts and wall hangings. Many of her pieces are award winners, and one of her quilts was the 1986 Wisconsin winner in the Great American Quilt Festival's Expressions of Liberty contest. This quilt was also chosen for the cover of a college history book.

One of the Carol's award-winning quilts, *Flying Geese in the Log Cabin*, is a variation of the Log Cabin theme with an appealing interplay of light and dark. The design is straightforward, but Carol's use of fabric scraps makes every block different and visually exciting. The light areas are heavily quilted with a feather design, using free-style machine-quilting techniques. For Carol this quilt is a medley of memories and family lore: The "logs" represent the quiltmaker's home, parts of which were constructed from a log barn built in 1867 by her great-grandfather's brother. The black triangles represent Canadian geese as they traverse the Horicon Flyway, a migration route near the Butzke's home.

Carol is a registered nurse and certified cardiopulmonary perfusionist, but she has chosen to spend time at home raising her family. She has always enjoyed working with her hands; in addition to quilting, which she took up in 1980, she knits, does cross-stitchery, crochets, and embroiders. Carol prefers to work a little every day on her quilting, but between the demands of her family, her responsibilities in three quilters' associations, and the time she spends judging and teaching quiltmaking, Carol usually works "fifteen minutes here, fifteen minutes there."

Flying Geese in the Log Cabin; *86 by 97 inches; all-cotton; machine pieced and machine quilted.*

Shadows in the Snow *(detail)*.

Glad Rag II; *34 by 54 inches; natural and synthetic fabrics; machine pieced.*

JOYCE MARQUESS CAREY

Bold geometric designs, stunningly rich textures, and a sense of spatial illusion are the hallmarks of Joyce Marquess Carey's dazzling wall quilts. Her enormous shimmering works can be as large as 11 by 25 feet, and she creates most of her quilts for specific locations in corporate offices or public buildings. For many years Joyce was a weaver and made complex wall pieces on a multiharness loom. Her weaving was widely acknowledged, and she was a professor of textile design at the University of Wisconsin. But her fascination with optical illusion, a desire to have a greater degree of freedom in her work, and the possibility of working in a larger scale led Joyce to become a quiltmaker. She began with a series of quilted pieces she calls Pliable Planes that are based on optical illusions. "I like to create the impression of depth in my work," the artist says, "even though my quilts are totally flat and not bent or curled as some appear to be. I like to create artwork that is fun to look at and that involves the viewer in visual games."

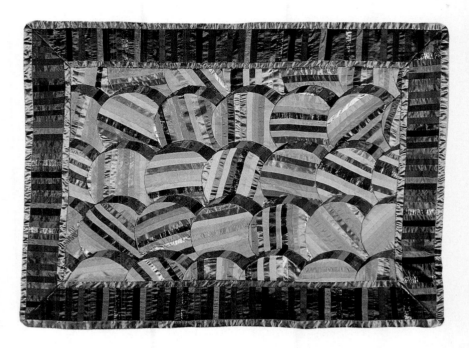

Tipping the Scales; 70 by 50 inches; various fabrics and metallic lamé; machine pieced and machine quilted.

The basic method of construction for Joyce's quilts is a variation of strip piecing. Using an industrial sewing machine, she sews hundreds of strips to a sturdy backing, usually heavy nylon, and uses no batting. The fabrics that form the face of the quilt can be silk, satin, velvet, brocade, lamé, or just about anything else. "I use anything that can be sewn and dry-cleaned," she says, but her favorites are theatrical fabrics, including metallics, because they add drama and light to a piece. Recently, Joyce has started to incorporate large prints or woven patterns into her work; she especially likes fabrics from Japanese kimonos and obis.

Tipping the Scales is one of her early pieces. It is a confection of shimmering and shiny fabrics that brings to mind a box filled with gaily wrapped, delectable bonbons. Even though *Reflections*, another of Joyce's quilts, makes use of fabrics with similar texture and sheen, it gives an entirely different impression. *Reflections* is more sedate, more measured, and more controlled than *Tipping the Scales*.

Many of this artist's wall quilts are irregularly shaped. *Sunshine and Shadow* is a lively amalgamation of polka dots flashed with bright color. The accordion shape not only adds extra character, it unexpectedly reinforces the various geometric forms that it frames. *Bon Kyoto*, another shaped piece, captures the flavor of Japan in a beautiful pieced medley of richly hued materials that includes snippets of kimono fabrics. *Glad Rag II*, one of a three-part series, is a glowing, twisting, curling ribbon. *Stepping Down* comprises the main elements of Joyce's work—shape, shimmer, and optical illusion—as well as a bit of wry social commentary, showing that pictorial abstraction can be used equally effectively within the overall context of her preferred mode of composition and design.

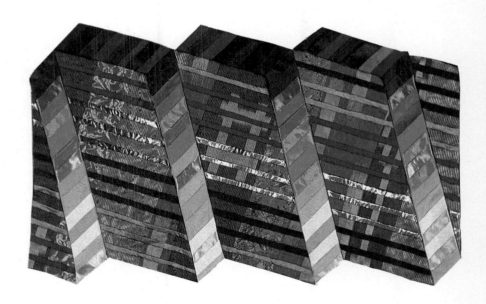

Bon Kyoto; 40 by 24 inches; silk and other fabrics; machine pieced and machine quilted.

Sunshine and Shadow; *66 by 46 inches; various
fabrics; machine pieced and machine quilted.*

Stepping Down; 70 by 32 inches; various fabrics;
machine pieced and machine quilted.

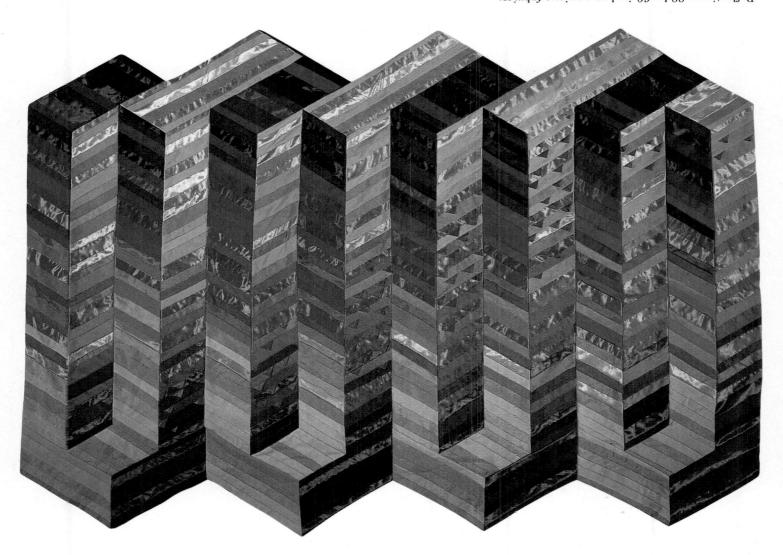

Reflections; 88 by 60 inches; various fabrics;
machine pieced and machine quilted.

Out of Bounds; 50 by 59 inches; cotton, cotton blends, and mother-of-pearl pieces; machine pieced and machine and hand quilted.

BARBARA LYDECKER CRANE

Barbara Lydecker Crane attended an exhibition of art quilts in 1980 and realized for the first time that quilts can be a serious art form. Relying on her fine arts background and basic sewing skills, Barbara immediately set about teaching herself to quilt. By 1981 she had completed her first wall quilt. Barbara admits that members of her quilt guild helped immensely during this learning period.

Barbara's subtle and striking designs carry with them an arresting yet elusive quality that encourages the viewer to delve into the mysteries her quilts present. "Birth, regeneration, and migration especially fascinate me," she says. "I am also drawn to the mystery of how life first came to be." This theme is exquisitely presented in her quilt *Internal Map*. Its delicate, predominantly blue grid creates a sense of wonder in a half-seen world of air, space, and water. The artist hints at the existence of life forms—birds and fish—in their unique elements, but she leaves their full delineation to the imagination. To Barbara the design represents "the geographies that maps can chart and the mysteries that maps cannot know. From these, diverse forms of life come into being." Barbara began this award-winning quilt with a strong image in her mind and a fast and enthusiastic sketch on paper. But she felt that it did not really come alive until she added paint to the images of the birds and fish. She says that the quilt was "a lot of tedious work during an extremely hot summer until I got to that point. I had tried to 'keep faith' in my original mental image, and suddenly—or finally—it all seemed worthwhile."

Out of Bounds, like many of this artist's quilts, presents both an abstract and a pictorial face. It is the eighth in a series of ten "window" quilts in which imagined landscapes are seen through doors or windows. Barbara says, "This quilt means freedom and hope. The architecture, which starts as a barrier to the viewer, gradually disappears toward the center of the quilt. This allows the birds to fly from the edges toward the center and thus through the window." The hand-quilted curved lines represent the flight paths of birds as they make their way to the freedom of the blue skies beyond the window. *Out of Bounds* is based on a simple block of eight pieces, which the artist reversed from left to right to create symmetry and perspective. To create the illusion of light spilling into the bottom border, Barbara used different colors of the same fabric. Hand-painted and hand-dyed fabrics also add to the impression that there is a landscape beyond the confines of the window panes.

Through its carefully considered gradations of color, Barbara's quilt *Change of View* represents both the passage of night into day and the progressive opening of a space. Although the piecing in this quilt is very simple, the choice of color and fabric was crucial to the effectiveness of the completed design. Barbara says that this was the time-consuming part of making the quilt.

Internal Map; *62 by 62 inches; cotton, seed pearls, and mother-of-pearl pieces; machine and hand pieced, and hand quilted.*

Change of View; *58 by 58 inches; all-cotton; machine pieced and machine quilted.*

Haitian Boat People I; *96 by 60 inches; cotton and cotton blends; machine pieced and machine quilted.*

MICHAEL A. CUMMINGS

Michael A. Cummings says that most of his quilts are narrative quilts that do not follow a traditional pattern. His quilts are rich in color and imagery, and his story ideas spring from many sources. This artist, who holds a degree in American art history, found his way to quilting making a banner for an event at the American Craft Museum in New York.

Michael's first quilt was a traditional Nine Patch pattern, and since then he has made more than twenty quilts, some traditional but most of his own design. Michael is inspired to make his colorful, asymmetrically pieced and appliquéd designs by news events, photo images, his own travels, and conversations with other quilters. His quilts shine with startlingly bright colors that jolt the viewer into paying attention to his narrative. He likes to work with cottons and cotton blends, partly because of their range of colors and also because of their durability.

Haitian Boat People is a triptych of quilts Michael made as an emotional reaction to the scenes of desperate Haitians that he saw nightly on television. The quilts symbolize the struggle of these people to escape a repressive government and the hardships that they have to endure to find a better way of life. In each of his quilts, hot bright colors, splashed against a dark background, reflect the vivid tones of tropical fish, plants, and animals. In his first Boat People quilt, a large and ungainly boat, densely packed with people, leaves the island, guided by a mermaid goddess of Haitian mythology. An all-seeing eye, which is a common convention of African-American quilts of the nineteenth and early-twentieth centuries, watches over all. The white figures that hover around the boat are also Haitian mythological figures; they are spirits with good and helpful intentions. The second Boat People quilt shows the boat at sea, surrounded by a colorful throng of sea creatures and spirits, including the mermaid goddess, helpful spirits, and angels. In the third quilt disaster strikes, and the boat overturns. The spirits fail to save the people, and the goddess sheds tears of sorrow.

African Jazz presents a simpler story than Michael's other quilts. The idea came from a poster showing three African musicians, and Michael created a fantasy environment with African overtones around that image. Even though his design started with the poster, the artist says, "everything else was just my imagination at work." He translated a black-and-white photo of three musicians in a corner of a smoke-filled bar into a wild and fantastic setting of high-contrast color that recalls Rousseau's naive images of jungles, plants, animals, and people. The juxtaposition of the figures and placement of their features are reminiscent of Picasso's work from the 1920s and 1930s. Michael's use of many different fabrics, with their clashing prints and divergent hues highlighted by textile paint, adds up to a certain raw and primitive power that makes the images in this quilt stunningly effective.

Haitian Boat People II; 95 by 60 inches; cotton and cotton blends; machine pieced and machine quilted.

African Jazz; 53 by 96 inches; cotton, cotton blends, beads, and buttons; machine pieced, reverse appliquéd, and hand quilted.

Hyperspace Dreams; *80 by 70 inches; cotton and cotton blends; machine and hand pieced, and hand quilted.*

JUDY B. DALES

Quilting started as a hobby for Judy B. Dales, a former schoolteacher, but it has now become a rewarding profession. About twenty years ago while she was living in London and expecting her first baby, Judy came across instructions in a magazine for making a patchwork quilt, and she says, "I was hooked immediately." Later, while her family was living in Germany, Judy taught herself everything there was to learn about quilting through trial and error, gradually perfected her stitching techniques, and developed a unique style. She finally went professional partially to support her fabric-buying habit.

Judy's first quilt was a modern version of Grandmother's Flower Garden and was eight years in the making. It started as a crib quilt and gradually expanded to fit a king-size bed, ultimately containing everything from British Liberty cottons to German dirndl fabrics to pieces of old maternity clothes and probably even some snips from her children's clothes. She has now made more than a hundred quilts, most of them wall hangings.

Blocks of colorful hexagons in an irregular arrangement cause *Kaleidoscopic Mutations* to give the impression that it is not quite static or finished. It seems as though it might be prone to erratic change or mutation. For Judy the quilt symbolizes the transient, kaleidoscopic nature of the world that is exceptionally beautiful but constantly changing. After completing the blocks for this quilt, the artist found she was tired of them and put them away for a while. When she took them out again, she was newly inspired and greatly enjoyed quilting the piece. She often makes blocks and then puts off assembling them.

Hyperspace Dreams is a dramatic multicolored collection of irregular quadrilateral shapes, each of which is different from the others and all of which seem to be exploding from a central point. Judy drew them freehand and filled each one with an eight-pointed star. She then surrounded the star blocks with inner and outer borders that give the illusion of depth. The quilt was part of an invitational challenge to create a piece using the theme of "dreamscapes," and Judy chose to depict the inner vision of a creative mind that is productive in sleep as well as when it is awake. "When I close my eyes, I see color and flashes of light," she says. "I suspect that when I sleep my subconscious mind forms the color and light into quilt blocks. This quilt shows designs flashing by at lightning speed—disappearing into the unknown from whence they came."

In The Pink is the second quilt in an ongoing series of abstract wave designs in which the title of the piece and the colors used are associated with a certain emotion. Judy says that pink is one of her favorite colors, and she sees it as representing gentleness, caring, and happiness. *The Blues* and *Mellow Yellow* are the telltale titles of other quilts in this award-winning series.

In The Pink; *60 by 52 inches; cotton and cotton blends; hand pieced and hand quilted.*

Kaleidoscopic Mutations; *80 by 70 inches; cotton and cotton blends; machine and hand pieced, and hand quilted.*

Night Blooming Cactus; *45 by 56 inches;*
all-cotton; machine pieced and machine quilted.

NANCY BRENAN DANIEL

Nancy Brenan Daniel uses traditional quilting techniques to present her own unique images of the Southwest. "There is so much romance and beauty in our American deserts," she says. Ideas for designs abound in this environment. Nancy's quilt *Night Blooming Cactus* is a splendid example of the way in which the quiltmaker captures the essence of the desert in fabric. The quilt is a jewellike interpretation of desert evenings when colors seem luminous and the air is heavy with the scent of cactus blossoms.

Many of Nancy's quilts are centrally organized, with the quilt border acting as part of the primary design and not simply as a frame for the center. "I don't work in traditional block constructions," she says. "My work is meant to be seen as a whole." Nancy begins each of her projects with a skeleton of an idea, and then the work tends to build itself organically. She often uses solid-color elements as a counterpoint to a distinctive combination of prints. "The concept leads me to the choice of fabrics," says the quiltmaker. Nancy plans her quilts in pieces and strips on a felt wall in her studio. For her the most exciting part of quiltmaking is designing and problem solving. The most difficult part is finishing the quilt.

Nancy's quilt *Christmas Cactus*, created as a medallion design, is the outstanding last project of a series called Prickly Pear Cactus. It has at its core a traditional Prickly Pear block, but from there the pattern becomes a grouping of turned concentric blocks. With sharp and colorful clarity, the blocks reflect the treacherous spines of the cactus and the enticing sweet red fruit that it bears. Nancy created superlative quilting designs to accentuate these two elements even further. The complex piecing and the elegant quilting took Nancy many hours to complete, but she refuses to speculate on the amount of time she spent on it. "I never measure my time on any of my quilts," she says. "I bet it would be depressing."

Nancy's grandmother, a lifelong quiltmaker, helped her learn her superb technique, but she has also learned a great deal on her own. Nancy started her first quilt when she was twelve, and she has yet to finish it. But since then she has made many wonderful quilts that have been seen in quilt shows, galleries, museums, books, calendars, and magazines. Nancy started teaching quiltmaking in 1971, and she now devotes almost all her time to quilts—designing them, making them, writing about them, judging them, or teaching other people how to make them. "I'm only discouraged by the limited number of hours in the day," she says.

Christmas Cactus; *56 by 56 inches; all-cotton; machine and hand pieced, and hand quilted.*

Night Blooming Cactus *(detail).*

Left Handed Compliments; *50 by 50 inches;*
all-cotton; machine pieced and machine quilted.

CHRIS WOLF EDMONDS

While acknowledging the impressive heritage of the patchwork patterns that have been passed down for many generations, Chris Wolf Edmonds also recognizes the responsibility of today's quiltmakers to add to that wealth of design rather than simply to repeat it. To explore a theme or concept to its fullest, Chris develops a series of quilts. My Funny Valentine is a series that was inspired by a song. For these quilts Chris used a lattice effect, a checkerboard pattern, and a similar color palette, but each quilt conveys a distinct message. Chris did not make drawings for these quilts or use patterns. "The idea developed in my mind," says the artist, "as pieces were added, stitched, sliced, and rearranged." In *My Funny Valentine II*, she used only hand-painted silk even though she usually prefers to work with cotton. The silk gives the finished piece a special luster, but Chris felt that she had to paint even the white areas to give the work an overall consistent texture.

Reconstruction is a startling and vivacious quilt that plays off colorful hand-painted silks against the dynamics of black and white and a checkerboard of solid colors to create the illusion of overlapping space. The quilt is not only a brilliant and effective design composition, but it is also a praiseworthy recycling project. The silk fabric in the isometric section of the design was originally part of another quilt that had never satisfied the artist, so Chris picked out the quilting and piecing stitches and reused the fabric in this new piece, appropriately titled *Reconstruction*.

Both *Reconstruction* and *Left Handed Compliments* are part of Chris's Electric Quilts series. The title comes from the fact that they are pieced and quilted by machine and because of the vivid color studies in their designs. In *Left Handed Compliments*, strips of intense, nearly complementary colors are combined and recombined to create a series of squares of various sizes that are then placed at angles within other squares to create an illusion of motion.

Fast Food was made for an invitational show called Americana Enshrined in Atlanta, Georgia. What better image of America could there be than our popular eating habits? The golden arches of McDonald's surmount realistic appliquéd renditions of favorite fast foods, while a patchwork of blocks depicts abstract versions of burgers and fries.

I Never Promised You a Rose Garden brings together a number of Chris's favorite elements in what she calls "a riotous growth of color in a thorny green background." Chris used hand-dyed fabrics that she strip pieced, cut, and arranged to blend the colors and values in the most effective manner. She then placed the color-toned circles in tilted squares within larger squares. The striped grounds of these second squares and the larger background join forces to produce a dynamic sense of motion and depth that seems to set the circles spinning.

My Funny Valentine II; *83 by 53 inches; all-silk; machine pieced, appliquéd, and machine quilted.*

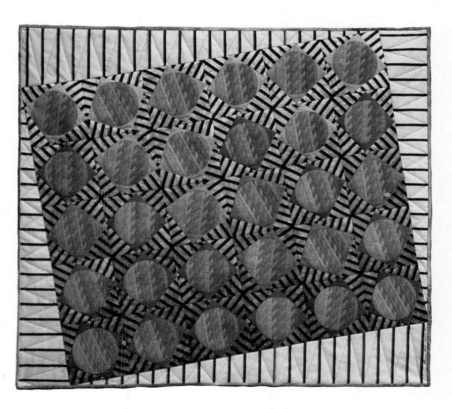

I Never Promised You a Rose Garden; *40 by 35 inches; all-cotton; machine pieced and machine quilted.*

CHRIS WOLF EDMONDS

Fast Food; *58 by 48 inches; all-cotton; machine pieced, appliquéd, and machine quilted.*

Reconstruction; *58 by 48 inches; cotton and silk;
machine pieced and machine quilted.*

My Funny Valentine IV; *58 by 53 inches;
all-cotton; machine pieced, appliquéd, and
machine quilted.*

Jewel Box III; *59 by 83 inches; all-cotton; machine pieced, appliquéd, and hand quilted.*

ANN FAHL

A nn Fahl tried out all the fiber arts before becoming a quilter. When she was in grade school, her grandmother taught her to knit and embroider. She then developed a passion for sewing. Ann earned a degree in textiles and clothing from the University of Wisconsin and went on to experiment with her own designs, using embroidery, weaving, and machine appliqué. In 1978 she signed up for a class in quiltmaking, hoping to improve her sewing skills, but Ann soon realized that she had found a medium that brought together her love of design, color, fabric, and stitchery. She took every class and workshop on quilting that she could find. "There had been a quilter inside of me, just waiting to come out," she says.

For Ann designing quilts is always a challenge. Sometimes an idea will emerge full-blown in an hour; other times months of thoughtful trial and error are necessary to achieve the desired effect. Her abstract designs are simple yet striking, with color playing a major role. One of Ann's favorite shapes is the triangle, and she always has a lot of them, all the same size, on hand. In her quilt *Squared Triangles*, the quiltmaker challenged herself to use up all the triangular scraps she had leftover from three previous projects without cutting any new pieces. The result is a symmetrical design that appears to be one large square laid on top of another—all composed of triangles. A circular quilting pattern and a black border dramatically set off the colors. Ann says that the quilt was basically designed on the floor where she arranged the triangles to find the pattern she wanted. While it took her about a week to piece the top, the quilting went more slowly, and the quilt took about four months to complete. "The whole creative process went so smoothly that this quilt was meant to be," she says.

Ann made two "jewel box" quilts during her "black-quilt period." She finds that black gives other colors an extra sparkle, and so she experimented with black and various color combinations to see what would happen. The first of this group of quilts, *Ann's Jewel Box*, bursts with exuberant color. The quilt is based on a block Ann saw in a magazine, but after she had completed twelve blocks and the center, the artist could not figure out how to finish the quilt. Finally she showed it to a class that she was teaching, and her students helped her come up with the right solution.

The design of *Jewel Box III* evolved from several wall hangings Ann had made and from her interest in creating something that would present gradations of bright color against black. The central star is pieced from hand-dyed fabrics. The summer day she dyed the fabric, Ann had eight dye pots sitting in her driveway and three four-year-old boys who wanted to help. "The amazing thing is that when the dying was complete not one of us was covered with bright green or purple," she says.

Squared Triangles; *49 by 49 inches; all-cotton; machine pieced and hand quilted.*

Ann's Jewel Box; *89 by 100 inches; cotton blends; machine pieced and hand quilted.*

Life in the Margins II: After Autumn; *51 by 65 inches; cotton and cotton blends; machine pieced, machine embroidered, appliquéd, and machine quilted.*

CARYL BRYER FALLERT

Caryl Bryer Fallert is a flight attendant who is also a full-time professional quilter. "If I am not working as a flight attendant or lecturing and teaching about quilts, I generally spend eight or more hours a day on my quilts." Caryl not only gives quilting workshops in the United States, but she has also talked about quiltmaking to audiences in Australia, New Zealand, and the People's Republic of China.

"For as long as I can remember, I have expressed myself through art," says Caryl, who makes wearable art as well as quilts. She learned to sew when she was ten and studied design and painting in college, but it took many years of painting, sewing, and working in other media before Caryl realized that she could best express her artistic vision with fabric. She has made more than a hundred quilts, many of them inspired by her travels. Caryl's designs are strikingly original, although she frequently puts her own rendition of a traditional block on the reverse side of a quilt.

For many of her quilts, Caryl employs a technique that makes ingenious use of three-dimensional tucks. Each of the tucks is a different color, and Caryl often twists them to create a stunning illusion of movement, light, excitement, and depth. *Checking Over the Rainbow V: Epicenter* is a vivid example of this technique. One-half-inch twisted tucks are incorporated into a pieced background, all using a full rainbow spectrum of color. The dramatic black-and-white jagged slash through the center represents the 1989 San Francisco earthquake, which occurred during the quilt's construction.

Chromatic Progressions: Autumn uses color gradations and twisted tucks in a series of interwoven arcs and around the border. To gain the appealing, muted color progressions, Caryl hand dyed the fabric. This gives the quilt an overall impression of a crisp, sunny day in autumn. *High Tech Tucks XV*, created as a triptych, owes its drama to the tucks that are twisted from side to side by the quilting stitches, subtly enhancing the shimmering sensation of movement that flows over the piece. A traditional Log Cabin block graces the back of this quilt. *Tropical Tucks II* inserts undulating tucks into a background created from a tropical print. The leaf shape of the background fabric is repeated in the quilting design on the outside border of the quilt.

Life in the Margins II: After Autumn takes its inspiration from the doodles that filled the margins of Caryl's school notebooks. The background is made of strips that are sewn together in related color groupings and then cut into diamonds and repieced. The quiltmaker machine embroidered the overlaid design that is cut from black fabric, but she used freehand quilting to echo the "doodle" design. The back of this quilt presents a dramatic contrast, with its bold and controlled design, loosely based on a Log Cabin block that was altered to echo the spiral of the front and provides a stark contrast to its glowing colors and free-flowing form.

Isosceles Garden; *76 by 85 inches; all-cotton; machine pieced and machine quilted.*

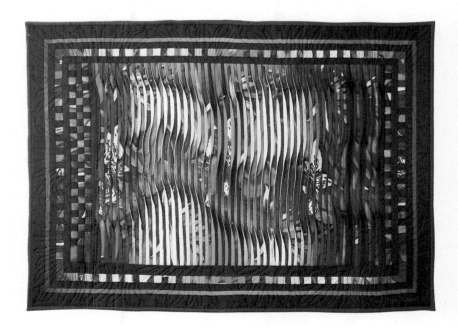

Tropical Tucks II; *57 by 40 inches; all-cotton; tucked, machine pieced, and machine quilted.*

CARYL BRYER FALLERT

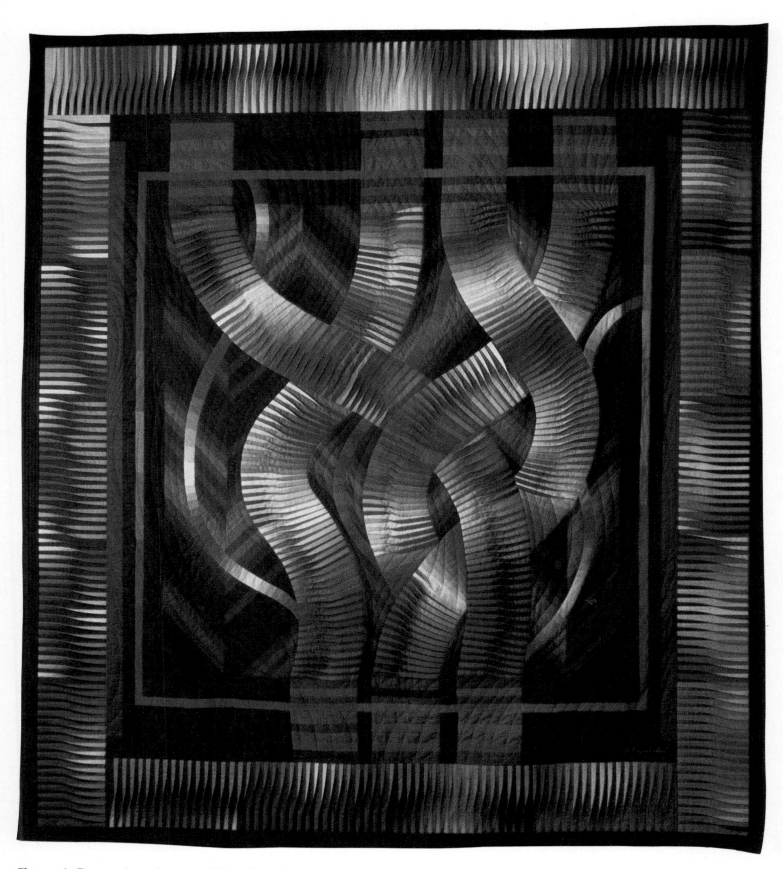

Chromatic Progressions: Autumn; *88 by 98 inches;
all-cotton; tucked, machine pieced, and machine
quilted.*

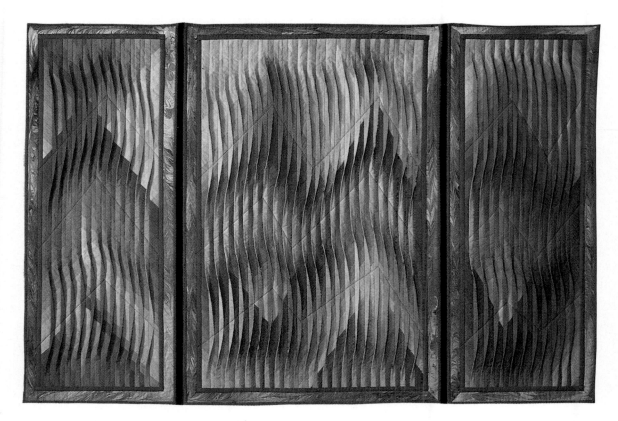

High Tech Tucks XV; *59 by 38 inches; all-cotton;*
tucked, machine pieced, and machine quilted.

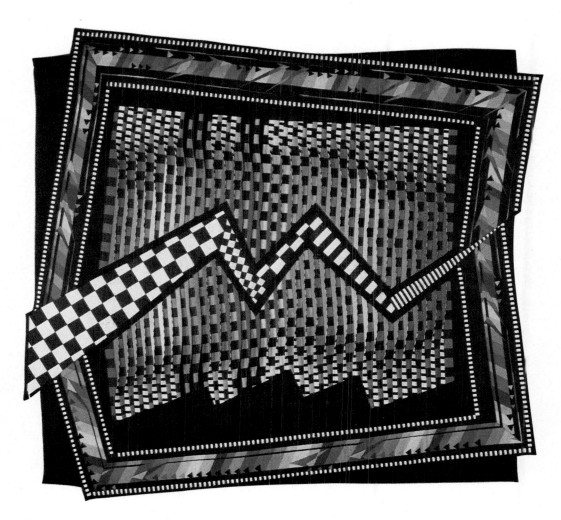

Checking Over the Rainbow V: Epicenter; *50 by*
43 inches; all-cotton; tucked, machine pieced, and
machine quilted.

Tree of Life; *69 by 86 inches; all-cotton; machine pieced and hand quilted.*

MARIANNE FONS

The Bicentennial sparked Marianne Fons's interest in quilts. She had embroidered for a number of years, but quilts appealed to her because quilting gave her "a much bigger product for the amount of time spent." Marianne convinced her local Iowa State University extension office to set up a quilting class. After completing that course, she took all the classes she could find, and within only a few years, Marianne had become a quilting teacher. She was surprised when her first quilt won a blue ribbon at the state fair; "I made so many mistakes," she says. The artist has now made dozens of award-winning quilted items inspired by nineteenth century quilt patterns, "but only a handful of large quilts," she says.

Tree of Life is a beautiful example of a traditional pattern enlivened by Marianne's own personal touches, such as setting the blocks on point. The rows of color symbolize changing seasons, from the cool blue tones of winter through the ruddy hues of fall, and a feather stitching pattern, which is one of the artist's favorites, flows around the border and joins in circles in the four-color blocks between the motif blocks. The quilt is a constant reminder of the beauty of life and of her own contribution to it.

For her *Lady Liberty* quilt and its companion, *World Peace*, Marianne drew inspiration from American medallion quilts of the eighteenth century. Like many of her own quilts, some of these historic quilts have blocks turned on point and floral borders. So that Marianne's quilts would be truly commemorative, she appliquéd words on them. She created *Lady Liberty* for the Great American Quilt Festival's Expressions of Liberty contest; it was the state winner. The artist wanted her quilt to be "beautiful, feminine, and grand, just like the Statue of Liberty." The face of Liberty is framed by Ocean Waves patchwork; other blocks used in the quilt also relate closely to its theme, including All Kinds, Brave New World, Hopes and Wishes, and Prosperity blocks. The floral border shows American Beauty roses, with trumpet flowers at the corners to herald the statue's hundredth birthday.

Marianne made her quilt *World Peace* for an international contest Visions of the World, and it was one of the winners. For this quilt Marianne used the same techniques she used for *Lady Liberty*; she also used many of the same fabrics. With a white dove of peace at the center and four repeated traditional blocks, World Without End, Friendship Links, Peace and Plenty, and Tree of Life, the quilt beautifully symbolizes the hope for world peace. The outer border is a ribbon twined through children's hands—a wonderful symbol of friendship among all people.

Lady Liberty; 72 by 72 inches; all-cotton; machine and hand pieced, appliquéd, reverse appliquéd, and hand quilted.

World Peace; 72 by 72 inches; all-cotton; machine and hand pieced, appliquéd, and hand quilted.

Multi-Facet; *39 by 39 inches; all-cotton; machine pieced and hand quilted.*

64

PAT BROOKS GASKA

Pat Brooks Gaska began quilting in hope of using up the piles of fabric scraps she had left over from making clothes. But after making between one- and two-hundred quilts of all sizes, her fabric collection is considerably larger than it was when she started, and she is more fascinated than ever by the design possibilities offered by quilts. Pat's first quilt was an intricately pieced Odd Fellow's Chain that she made for her mother; she had intended to hand quilt it but was so frustrated after the piecing was completed that she machine quilted it instead.

Pat's quilt *Jeweled Boxes* really looks three dimensional. The quilt suggests complexity competing with tranquility in the dislocation of the design as the orderly pattern seems to break up and disappear. But the solid areas provide a balance to the smooth range of color in the octagons that balance on an underlying grid. Quilted within each small octagon is an eight-pointed star, and that motif is carried over into the plain white area to enhance the pattern. Even though the artist found the design easy, the construction proved to be a problem and she had to work out new methods as the quilt top progressed.

Multi-Facet grew out of a workshop that explored the concentric patterns of mandalas as they appear in nature and in the art of many cultures. Pat drafted the intriguing design that is circular within a square by using a paper-folding technique. The artist sees the design as whole, quiet, and contemplative. She chose the colors as she went along, letting the quilt itself guide her choices. For this quilt Pat used solid rather than patterned fabrics because she did not want to detract from the complexity of the design. For this reason she also used only outline quilting, except in the corner areas where the stitching is meant to echo the shape of the design.

Working out the logistical problems inherent in a large medallion quilt led the artist to explore the medallion further in her quilt *Geometrics Medallion*. Pat was very excited as she laid out and completed successive sections of this quilt. For her the quilting was anticlimactic in comparison to the piecing. The work has a vibrancy and energy not usually found in medallion quilts, and the colors form a dynamic blend that contributes to its three-dimensional effect.

Pat used to be a full-time quilter, but now she works as a liturgy coordinator for a church. She still commits one full workday each week to quilting, allowing herself no lunch dates, no doctor's appointments, and no other interruptions. She also quilts in the evenings and on weekends. Her quilts, which have appeared in many invitational and juried shows, as well as books, magazines, and other publications, are in many private collections, and her liturgical vestments and banners, many of which employ traditional quilting techniques, are owned by many Wisconsin churches.

Geometrics Medallion; *88 by 88 inches; all-cotton; machine pieced and hand quilted.*

Jeweled Boxes; *73 by 48 inches; all-cotton; machine pieced and hand quilted.*

Armadillo Highway; *72 by 84 inches; cotton blends; machine pieced, appliquéd, and hand quilted.*

HELEN GIDDENS

Most of Helen Giddens's quilts are based on doodles. "I doodle all the time. The ones I like end up as quilts," she says. Helen's lively doodles, such as her quilt *Snake*, are often inspired by memories. "I grew up in the south-central part of the country where there are always plenty of snakes slithering around," she says. "They mean a lot of different things to different people, but personally I like their movement." The snake in the center of this quilt is set in motion by the swirl quilting and the pieces of fabric that follow its sinuous form. Helen's decision to use wavy rather than straight edges adds even more snakelike motion to the quilt.

Although no two pieces in her quilts are the same size and shape, Helen's piecing technique is actually very simple. She draws the design, traces it, numbers and color codes the pattern pieces, and then cuts. "It's really like doing a puzzle," she says.

Helen liked the rattles in her *Snake* so much that she decided to arrange a composition of rattles. The final grouping of four reminded her of her family—herself and her three children—so she named the quilt *Rattle Family*. The print fabric is a 1970s chintz that Helen had on hand. She uses mostly scraps for her quilts, culling through her collection to see what she has that is appropriate for a design.

Helen's quilt *Armadillo Highway* is also based on events from her own life. Before she made this quilt, Helen had not made a quilt for about six years. But during a major move from Oklahoma to Texas, she saw many dead snakes and armadillos along the highway. Her quilt design includes the images of these animals. The sand colors of the background fabric represent the dry, hot summer landscape; the wild animal prints suggest the untamed countryside through which she drove; the red armadillos represent the dead ones; and the checkered print hints at the marks of tire treads. While most of her earlier quilts had been block patterns, this quilt was conceived as a whole picture, even though the images were abstracted and some of the elements were repeated. Although the subject matter represents a sad fact of life on the highway, Helen has created a sympathetic and appealing composition.

Helen began to quilt when she was sixteen. She was inspired by a New York Beauty quilt that her grandmother had made for her parents' anniversary. She made her first quilt for her high-school sweetheart; it was an original design that included a heart and their names. After that first quilt, Helen, who also paints and makes silk screen prints, made many quilts based on traditional patterns. Recently she has begun to create her own designs, often based on her doodles. Even though Helen grew up playing under the quilting frame where her mother was working, she is basically self-taught. Helen's quilts have won many awards, including state winner of the Memories of Childhood crib-quilt contest sponsored by the Museum of American Folk Art in 1988.

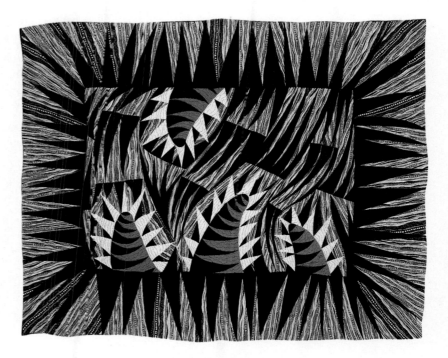

Rattle Family; *60 by 45 inches; cotton blends; machine pieced and machine quilted.*

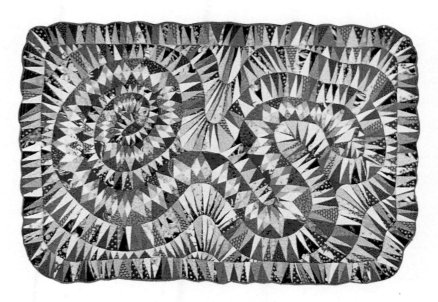

Snake; *110 by 70 inches; cotton blends; machine pieced and machine quilted.*

Bitty's Dream; *62 by 85 inches; all-cotton;*
machine pieced and hand quilted.

HOPE GREEN

Miami letter carrier Hope Green says that she truly loves every step in the quilting process. The license plates on her and her husband's cars read I QUILT and I QUILT 2. "They are a wonderful way to meet quilters when we're traveling," she says. For Hope crocheting, needlepoint, and knitting did not seem to fill the bill, but once she found a quilt pattern that she loved, she knew she had found the right craft. The pattern was Dogwood. This tree does not grow in South Florida and "perhaps that is why I wanted a quilt full of dogwood blossoms," she says. Piecing *Dogwood Memories* consumed Hope's life for the next five months; even her lunch breaks were devoted to finishing the top. When the quilt was completed, Hope had the pleasure of seeing it awarded second prize in a show, and her enthusiasm for quilting was confirmed. This quilt also made Hope a quilt teacher. She had created a "signature block" on the back of the quilt in which she embroidered the quilt's name, her name, and the year. When she completed the quilting on the front, she left the back unstitched around the embroidery. Other quilters at the show were so intrigued by her technique that they immediately asked for lessons in how to do it. This signature block became her logo, and Hope puts one on each of her quilts.

Sometimes the artist creates her own designs, and sometimes she works with traditional ones. *Celtic Rose*, a stunning adaptation of a quilt Hope saw at a show, blends original and traditional motifs. The blocks are set on point, and the design in each block is different. The quiltmaker altered the edge triangles to fit the new format and used a bias appliqué throughout. Heavy quilting gives the work a wonderful sense of depth. The artist says that the quilt, which was pieced while she was recovering from a back injury, helped her get through the long, slow healing process.

The sprightly floral explosion that is *Bitty's Dream* actually started out to be place mats. The artist had bought Rose Fever squares and border fabric to make place mats, but in a dream she saw them in full color as part of a Triple Irish Chain quilt. The next day Hope rushed back to the store to buy the coordinating prints and solids to make her dream a reality. Hope made this quilt in her new workroom where, she says, it was a joy to use her new cutting table that is the right height to work over with no backache.

In addition to large quilts, Hope has made three 28-by-21-inch quilts for her hundred-year-old doll bed. She plans to make a total of 12 doll quilts. When she is drafting patterns and piecing, Hope tends to work intensively for long periods at a time, but once there is a quilt on her frame, her goal is a minimum of a half hour of quilting each day. But that can easily turn into three hours, even after a ten-hour workday. "My husband loves to see me stitching," she says, "because it brings peace and fulfillment and happiness to the whole house."

Celtic Rose; 81 by 81 inches; all-cotton; appliquéd and hand quilted.

Bitty's Dream (detail).

Mr. and Mrs. Cottontail; *35 by 44½ inches;*
all-cotton; machine pieced, appliquéd, and hand
quilted.

ROSIE GRINSTEAD

Rosie Grinstead grew up with quilts. Two of her great-grandmothers quilted, and their handiwork was well used and well loved by Rosie's family. Her first attempt at quiltmaking was a crib quilt that her mother had started for her. Rosie finished it about thirty years ago when she was pregnant with her first child. "I had no help then," she says, "so it is full of mistakes." Her interest in quilting was rekindled during the Bicentennial, when she was chairperson of a crafts boutique that sold patchwork items. She began to learn more on her own and from quiltmakers she met through her guild membership, and started making crib quilts for her family and friends. It was not long until Rosie began designing her own quilts and teaching.

Her triple-prize-winning quilt *Spring Beauties* is a wonderful medley of more than a hundred different fabrics cut into 2,600 pieces. It is based on the traditional Block pattern, but this quilt is arranged in an original manner. It was made almost entirely from scrap print fabrics that the artist had on hand, although Rosie says she traded for a few pieces of material to keep color groupings consistent. The quiltmaker started *Spring Beauties* as a sampler for a lecture on scrap quilts, but she quickly expanded the design beyond her original intention. Rosie says she had a lot of fun making the quilt top because the fabric arrangement was so random, but the elaborate and beautiful Feather and Hearts quilting required four or five a hours a day over several months to complete.

Even though *Broken Star Medallion* is based on a traditional Broken Star, Rosie had to elongate the center and make the borders extra wide to fit an antique bed with unusual dimensions. Rosie planned this quilt as a college graduation present for her daughter. But the meticulous and intricate quilting required nine months of work, and she finally finished it a year after the graduation on a weekend her daughter announced her engagement.

Mr. and Mrs. Cottontail is an adorable crib quilt. The four appliquéd rabbit blocks (two boys and two girls) are surrounded by a tulip border, with the quilting behind the tulips reflecting the picket fences in the blocks. The sashing is quilted with hearts. This design combines a commercial pattern for the applique with an original border design. The artist particularly enjoys making crib quilts and has made about thirty. She now designs crib quilts for a pattern company, but when she designs a pattern that is especially appealing to her, she may keep it for herself to use in workshops and lectures.

Quiltmaking is Rosie's full-time occupation, and she works nearly every day. During the day she designs and pieces in her basement studio; she quilts in the late afternoon. "I find the actual quilting very relaxing," she says, "so I really look forward to that." The artist is a member of six quilters' associations, and her award-winning quilts have appeared in juried and invitational shows around the country.

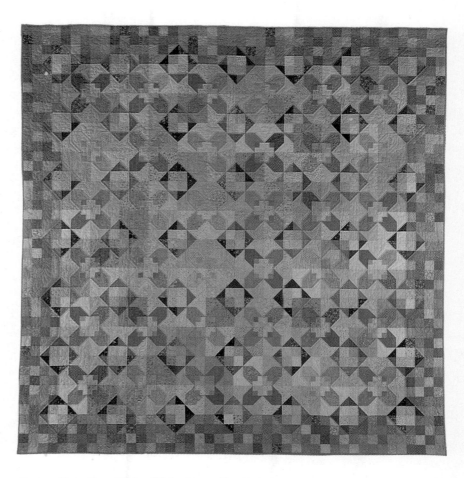

Spring Beauties; *86 by 86 inches; all-cotton; machine pieced and hand quilted.*

Broken Star Medallion; *100 by 120 inches; all-cotton; machine pieced and hand quilted.*

Indigo; *52 by 70 inches; all-cotton; machine pieced and hand quilted.*

JANE HALL

J ane Hall started quilting when she was living in Hawaii. She wanted an Hawaiian quilt and found that the only way for her to get one was to make it herself. She was already skilled at needlepoint, embroidery, and other needle crafts, but there were few classes in quilting available, so she read books, watched Hawaiian quilters, bought a pattern, and began to teach herself. When she returned to the mainland, she took every workshop that she could to learn more techniques.

That first full-size Hawaiian quilt has led to eight more large quilts and about sixty smaller wall hangings and crib quilts. Jane's quilts have hung in national, regional, and local shows and won many awards from honorable mention to best of show. Initially, the artist interpreted traditional patterns with contemporary colors and settings. Now, she experiments with shapes, strips, and ways to use color in both traditional and more innovative forms. Adaptations of traditional designs are still a challenge, and her current specialty involves variations on Pineapple and Log Cabin patterns.

Indigo is a traditional Pineapple quilt to which Jane has added her own unique touches. She made the pineapple design larger and added extra rows of blue to emphasize the pineapple figures. Part way through assembling the blocks, she realized that the fabric in the large triangular corners of each block could be placed so that the pattern appeared to swirl, so she resewed the blocks to achieve this exciting effect. The quilt, she says, showed her how playing with fabric can lead to changes in original plans and how a quilt can grow and change while it is being made.

Princess Feather and Rising Star combines Mariner's Compass pieced blocks and Princess Feather appliqué. It is an adaptation of an antique quilt made in about 1850. Jane saw a photograph of this quilt more than twenty years ago and thought it was the most beautiful quilt she had ever seen. Jane made her quilt with the help of her Friendship Quilt group. When it was her turn to choose the quilt that the group would make, she drafted the pattern, chose the fabric, and set the quilters to making the 20 Mariner's Compasses that were necessary. Then Jane appliquéd Princess Feathers over all the block joins, made the appliquéd borders, and finally added the swirly wave quilting block by block to give the quilt a greater sense of movement. The amount of appliqué was daunting, she says, ''but by plodding on it got finished. My needle turning certainly improved by the last of the 31 feathers.''

Galaxy is an eight-pointed star quilt based on the Le Moyne Star pattern. Its 16 blocks are butted together with no sashing so that secondary patterns are formed. Each star appears to be made from different fabric, but all were cut from different areas of the same eye-catching piece of jungle fabric. The quilting design emphasizes the stars as well as the areas created by the setting.

Galaxy; *34 by 34 inches; all-cotton; hand pieced and hand quilted.*

Princess Feather and Rising Star; *84 by 101 inches; all-cotton; hand pieced, appliquéd, and hand quilted.*

Safari Blizzard; *54 by 78 inches; all-cotton; machine pieced, appliquéd, and hand quilted.*

BARBARA OLIVER HARTMAN

Barbara Oliver Hartman uses traditional techniques to make quilts that pack an emotional punch. Her first quilt was based on a simple Amish design, but most of the quilts Barbara now makes are her own designs. Some employ Native American imagery; others have delicate overtones of social protest through which the artist expresses her concerns about human rights.

Barbara's quilt *Call Me Al* addresses the despair and agony caused by the apartheid system in South Africa. The specific inspiration for the quilt was Paul Simon's song of the same name and his Graceland concert. Barbara Hartman had many good ideas for this quilt, but she found that they only came together after she had seen an exhibition of Picasso's paintings and was inspired to put her images together in a powerful and unusual manner. Barbara collected black-and-white print fabrics for about a year before starting this quilt. The absence of color underscores the drama of her design, and her use of the traditional techniques of direct appliqué, embroidery, and hand quilting offsets the quilt's stark contemporary look. Barbara says she found both the concept and design of this quilt exciting to work on.

Safari Blizzard, which is part of a Quilt National worldwide tour, blazes with contrasting colors that add to its message of protest against social policies in South Africa. Barbara used colors she enjoys wearing and working with in this quilt, but here her favorite colors also have specific meanings. The magenta and the orange in the central field of the quilt each represent a race, one dominating one side of the quilt and one the other; the gold section in the middle is an invisible wall holding the two sides apart. A number of disparate images flow throughout the border, highlighted by stitching that presents still other images. To make this quilt, Barbara used traditional methods in a nontraditional way. For her the most difficult part of this pieced and appliquéd work was using metallic thread to hand quilt the overlapping concentric circles of the center part of the quilt.

"*Fuego en la Noche* was quite a lot of fun to make," Barbara says. She used fabrics from Australia, Japan, Indonesia, South America, and Africa, many of which are hand dyed or hand painted. Many of the fabrics have a vibrant tropical flavor, and every piece of material used in the quilt has some black in it. "Black with the bright colors seems hot to me," Barbara says. "I am reminded of a hot, tropical summer night that is lit in the distance with bright flashes of unknown origin." The center portion, based on curved two-patch blocks, is pieced, and not one of the blocks is repeated. The enigmatic forms that float mysteriously through the solid black border are all hand painted as well.

Barbara has made about a hundred quilts and wall hangings. She is a member of four quilters' associations and the American Craft Council.

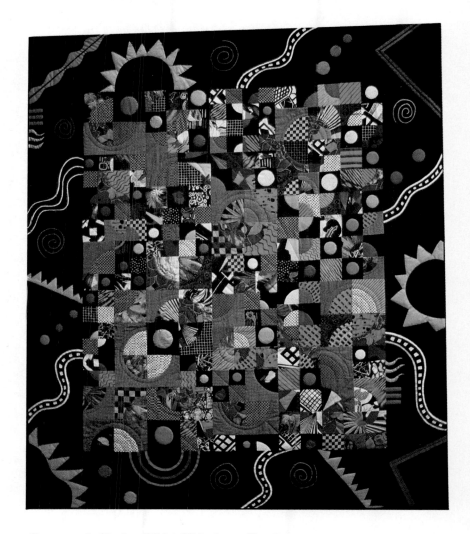

Fuego en la Noche; *77 by 87 inches; all-cotton; machine pieced and hand quilted.*

Call Me Al; *64 by 62 inches; all-cotton; hand appliquéd, hand embroidered, and hand quilted.*

Memories; *64 by 82 inches; all-cotton; machine
pieced and hand quilted.*

DIXIE HAYWOOD

Dixie Haywood gives standard patterns her own personal touch and comes up with innovative quilts that resonate with excitement and color. Her first quilt was a satin whole-cloth crib quilt that she made for her first child. She did not make another for about fifteen years, but since that second quilt, she has made about a hundred pieces. The artist, who is mostly self-taught, has an extensive background in quiltmaking, and in addition to writing regularly about quilting techniques and design, she teaches quilting classes. Her quilts with their engaging designs created "from everywhere and nowhere," as Dixie says, have been honored in many shows and competitions throughout the country.

Memories is a beautiful and meticulous example of a traditional pieced Pineapple quilt. It was a project that simply happened: The artist was organizing a box of fabric scraps that had been piling up for years, and she says, "one thing led to another." The quilt is a collection of fond remembrances; every scrap brings back memories of where the fabric was purchased, where the artist lived when she first used it, and which other quilts she made with the fabric. The most difficult part of the quilt was keeping the myriad of colors straight, since the color of each block was determined by the adjacent blocks.

Ojo de Dios, or "Eye of God," is also based on a Pineapple block, but the artist added graphic elements to make the pattern unique. The four interior designs, centered on the red diamond, represent the Eye of God that is frequently seen in Mexican folk design. Dixie made this quilt for an invitational challenge and had to use materials chosen from a group of fabrics furnished by one of the sponsors. The design also had to be made up of half solids and half prints. The quiltmaker pieced this quilt on a removable foundation, with the design formed by preplanned color changes within the basic block. Although the design was complex, Dixie found the hardest part was working out a quilting pattern that would enhance the graphic focus of the quilt.

Dixie's abstract and dramatic quilt *Redcubes* seems three dimensional. It is the artist's first large-scale exploration of the technique of same-fabric crazy quilting. The textures of the "tops" of the cubes and the rectangles are achieved by Crazy Quilt piecing of the same fabric overlaid by quilting. The quilting in the ditch reinforces the piecing, emphasizing the texture. Dixie chose materials that accentuated the dimensional effect, but she found that she had to requilt a large part of this piece because the original quilting for the navy background did not work. Her stitching pattern proved to be far too elaborate for the graphics of the quilt, so she reworked it in a simple linear design to increase the sense that the other elements are floating in the depths of space.

Ojo de Dios; *36 by 26 inches; all-cotton; machine pieced and hand quilted.*

Redcubes; *69 by 84 inches; cotton, cotton blends; machine pieced, appliquéd, and hand quilted.*

Basket and Bows; *92 by 106 inches; all-cotton;
machine pieced and hand quilted.*

ESTHER A. HERSHBERGER

E sther A. Hershberger comes from an Amish background. "I have been around quilting all my life," she says. She started making her own clothes when she was 11 years old, but she did not make a quilt until after the birth of her first son. "I had been working full time until then," she says, "and when I left to have a baby, I realized that I wanted to be more occupied and quilting seemed a logical choice."

The artist often uses traditional Amish patterns, but she also peruses quilt books and magazines for new ideas. Esther prefers traditional designs, but she likes to add her own combinations of colors. This quiltmaker rarely uses prints, preferring glowing groups of solids in keeping with Amish tradition. She frequently uses white in her quilts because it is a striking contrast to her other color choices and provides a showcase for her spectacular quilting.

Kansas Wheat is a whole-cloth quilt in which superlative stitching highlights the intricate and graceful wheat design that entwines the central medallion and the inner border. The breathtaking traditional design on the quilt top was marked by another woman and quilted by Esther. The fact that this quilt is all-white is a break with tradition, since earlier Amish quilters rarely used white, preferring dark colors that are easier to keep looking clean.

Basket and Bows, a pretty springlike quilt, entices the viewer with its simple charm and meticulous detail. It is also a deviation from an established tradition in Amish quilting. Although the pattern itself is frequently found in American quilts, for many years Amish quilters did not use appliqué. Now, appliquéd quilts are becoming more common among some groups of Amish quilters. Esther feels that appliqué has become more acceptable because there are some designs, such as these elegantly curved basket handles, that can only be executed with appliqué.

In a striking contrast of white and color, *Flying Geese in the Cabin* combines two patterns, Log Cabin, which is one of the artist's favorites, and Flying Geese. The border colors echo the darker blocks, and the cable quilting around the border, which is interrupted only by the quiltmaker's initials and the date of the quilt, adds a delightful final touch. Like all of Esther's work, this quilt is made of all-cotton fabrics because "they quilt much nicer." She always preshrinks the fabric before she begins cutting and piecing so that there will be no surprises once the quilt is finished and in use.

Esther, whose lovely quilts are award winners at the county fairs, has made more than twenty quilts on which she has done both piecing and quilting, but she has made about a hundred Log Cabins as well as many other patterns that other quilters have quilted for her. There are many Amish women in her community who love to quilt but do not like to piece. Esther provides them with pieced tops, they quilt them, and Esther markets the finished product.

Flying Geese in the Cabin; *103 by 103 inches; all-cotton; machine pieced and hand quilted.*

Kansas Wheat; *92 by 108 inches; all-cotton; hand quilted.*

Don't Tie Me Down; *56 1/2 by 69 inches; all-cotton; hand pieced and hand quilted.*

MARY KAY HITCHNER

Mary Kay Hitchner became interested in quilting in the late 1960s, during what she calls her "crewel embroidery and needlepoint stage." Books on quilting were not readily available in bookstores then, so she scoured libraries for the quilting classics, subscribed to quilters' newsletters, and used the information she had gathered to make a series of small projects, including several quilted pillows. Finally, she was encouraged enough with her progress to make her first quilt and chose a Tumbling Blocks pattern. The superbly constructed and pleasantly toned quilts she now makes blend old and new designs and techniques. Mary Kay adapts and manipulates familiar and traditional quilt blocks in exhilarating new ways. She uses only printed fabrics that provide an exciting sense of texture, depth, and visual tension. Her quilting patterns, which she designs specifically for each quilt, contribute a sensation of movement while enhancing the three-dimensional quality of her work.

The artist found that workshops in design techniques and color were particularly helpful as she developed her skills. She especially enjoyed classes that encouraged quilters to get past making copies of traditional patterns to design their own original work. Mary Kay is constantly experimenting and growing as a designer. Her inspiration for designs comes from many sources, not the least of which is antique quilts. *Tulips Aglow: 1830s Revisited* is an artistic combination of designs that were popular in the 1830s. A Feathered Star with swirling tulips acts as a central medallion. It is surrounded by borders of Sawtooth and Nine Patch set on point; an outside border in a repeat strip further carries out the tulip theme in softly glowing colors.

Don't Tie Me Down was the first quilt that Mary Kay entered in a competition; it won second prize. This original design is loosely based on the traditional Bow Tie block, but Mary Kay adjusted the square block shape to create an overall lattice pattern and then pieced it to achieve the impression of flying three-dimensional bow-tie stars. This perception is enhanced by spirals of stitching. The dilemma, the artist says, was to make the design look both old and modern at the same time. This happy fusion of color, design, and technique provided the ideal solution.

Campgrounds is an irregularly shaped quilt inspired by a piece of fabric printed with an impressionistic grove of trees. The minute she saw the fabric, Mary Kay thought of camping and the canoe trips she had made. She reinforced this impression by surrounding the scene with pieced blocks representing old-fashioned tents nestled among the trees in a campground. Outline quilting around the trees brings them out from the background, and a Japanese filler design overlays the delicate hues of the blocks. Appropriately enough, Mary Kay worked on this quilt over one summer while watching her children swim.

Tulips Aglow: 1830s Revisited; *54½ by 54½ inches; all-cotton; machine pieced and hand quilted.*

Campgrounds; *36 by 32 inches; all-cotton; machine and hand pieced, and hand quilted.*

81

Vase of Flowers; *38½ by 50 inches; cotton, silk, and beads; hand appliquéd with channel and padded trapunto, embroidered, and hand quilted.*

LOIS K. IDE

During the bicentennial year, members of the National Council of State Garden Clubs decided to make a quilt for their president. Lois K. Ide was asked to make a block for the state of Ohio, and she has been making quilts ever since. Lois has also contributed blocks to five other national quilts, two of which are now owned by museums. She learned sewing from her mother, a professional dressmaker, who taught her many wonderful quilting techniques that were used in the 1800s. ''She taught me how to see and how to interpret what I see into new designs,'' Lois says.

Lois can find designs for quilts almost any place she looks. She has been inspired by traditional quilt patterns, nature, ceramics, paintings, greeting cards, and even wallpaper. But no matter what kind of design she is working on, Lois prefers to work with natural materials—silk, cotton, and wool.

Lois's quilt *Vase of Flowers* is a rich bouquet of tulips, gladiolus and lilies that was inspired by a piece of antique lacquer work, which itself was influenced by Persian decorative painting. The flowers in the quilt are Lois's favorites, and the red copihue vine is the national flower of Chile, where she spent a pleasant visit several years ago. The quiltmaker learned the three-dimensional technique she used for the buds of the gladiolus from her mother who had used it for special decorations on hats and dresses. The trapunto techniques (channel, padded, and stuffed) are similar to those used in Baltimore Album quilts of the 1800s, as is the embroidery. For Lois the most difficult part of this quilt was making it in the short time period allowed by the competition for which it was made. But she managed to complete all the intricate detail for this lovely quilt in about three months.

Her quilt *Amish Lancaster Rose* is based on an Amish Diamond design, but Lois added her personal touch of appliquéd Lancaster roses, which Amish quilters admire and include in their commercial work but do not use in their own homes. The appliqués are padded trapunto, which gives extra depth and texture to the design. The deep, rich colors of the quilt are typical of Amish work and so are the quilting patterns. This quilt was made for the quiltmaker's son, who admired the Amish people and their way of life. Although he saw the quilt started, he died unexpectedly before it was finished. For more than a year, Lois was unable to work on the quilt, but she eventually finished it as a tribute to her son.

Lois's quilts have won both national and international recognition, and have been featured in many books. One of her pieces was selected by UNICEF as a potential greeting card, and in 1989 she was the recipient of an Ohio Arts Council grant. The quiltmaker, who has been teaching quilting since 1978, says that she is thrilled to win awards and recognition with her quilts but she believes that teaching is her greatest quilting accomplishment.

Amish Lancaster Rose; *91¹/₂ by 91¹/₂ inches; all-cotton; machine pieced, appliquéd, and hand quilted.*

Vase of Flowers (*detail*).

Four Block Park; *54 by 62 inches; all-cotton;*
machine pieced, machine embroidered,
appliquéd, and machine quilted.

DAMARIS JACKSON

When Damaris Jackson, who holds a degree in music and dance, decided that she wanted to make a quilt, she made it completely on her own. "I didn't consult books or people and so, of course, I ran into many technical problems," she says. "But I also came up with many ideas." Damaris's first quilt is a collection of appliquéd animals and people done in corduroy. It led her into an ongoing flurry of quiltmaking. For two years she supported herself by making hundreds of quilts and selling them at craft fairs. But once her work started gaining recognition, Damaris began to concentrate on intrinsic artistic elements rather than on production. She now makes only a few complex quilts a year.

Four Block Park combines whimsical quilted line drawings with elements of traditional patchwork. The playful scenes of events and activities that you might see on a walk through the park provide a strong narrative element. They are based on pen-and-ink drawings that Damaris originally made without a quilt in mind. She hand guided a sewing machine, using a darning foot to make the simple continuous lines stitched in white against the black background.

Lines from the Park is another quilt in the Park series. It was inspired by a 65-acre park near Damaris's home. A wide border encompasses both abstract and realistic stitched drawings that are put together like a Crazy Quilt to suggest the fragments of lives, events, and perspectives that make up the essence of a park. Wind and landscape lines are quilted in. The indentations in the center are intended to keep the central portion from becoming too much of a framed focal point. They draw the eye back out to the activities depicted in the surrounding border. The stitching on the central panel and along the edges goes through both sides of the quilt, but the intricate drawing stitches and the embroidery of the border are seen only on the quilt top. On the back of this quilt, which is intended to be two-sided, there is an Amish Bars design with an added focus on trees. Damaris snipped away the leaves on two of the corner trees so that the bright layer of fabric below may be seen. Then she stitched around their edges for stability but did not turn them under.

Not Everyone Swims Laps is a celebration of individual choice as well as an appreciation of different environments. Lap swimmers are stitched into the pieced rectangles that form narrow lanes, and the people not swimming laps are stitched cavorting in the large watery areas and on the splashlike flowers. The artist's trips to the YMCA to go swimming, "sometimes doing laps, and sometimes not," she says, and the fabrics themselves inspired this quilt. "I enjoyed the challenge of making a quilt suggest a swimming pool," she says, "and I am planning several more quilts on the same theme." In this piece the stitching takes second place to the texture and colors of the fabrics. "My next piece in the series will focus on more impact with the stitching."

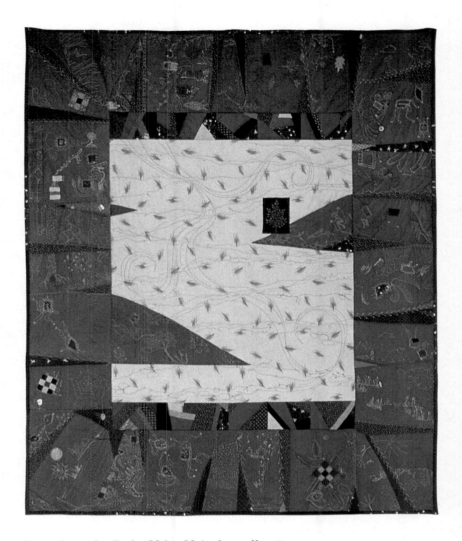

Lines from the Park; *83 by 98 inches; all-cotton and decorative objects; machine pieced and machine quilted.*

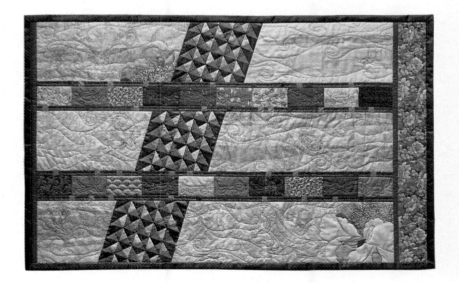

Not Everyone Swims Laps; *63 by 39 inches; all-cotton; machine pieced, machine embroidered, appliquéd, and machine quilted.*

Contact; *50 by 50 inches; cotton and cotton blends; machine pieced and machine and hand quilted.*

ANN JOYCE

With two little children to care for, it is sometimes difficult for Ann Joyce to find time to work. But this widely exhibited, self-taught artist, whose work is included in many public collections, manages to work on her quilts every day: "I make the time," she says, "either when the children are asleep, or sometimes I let them play in the room with me." Ann has made about one hundred and fifty quilts.

Many of Ann's quilts are traditional block quilts with sashing that forms an organizing grid, but the designs within the blocks come straight out of the artist's vivid imagination. Ann often uses personal experiences as starting points for the imagery in her quilts. She is an avid reader, and some of her designs are inspired by books that she has read. She hopes that her fabric designs convey the feelings engendered by written words. Her quilts are visual analogues for the mental images created by her reading.

Contact, a fictional account by Carl Sagan about making contact with extraterrestrials, lead Ann to design a quilt of the same name. The quilt has an otherworldly quality that reflects the book, but the quiltmaker says it also speaks to her of the possibilities of an afterlife. The quilt is one of a series of four ingenious asymmetrical designs that uses the same set of blocks, but in each quilt these elements are recombined and reworked. *Contact* was the first quilt in which Ann used patterned fabrics; previously she had used solid colors. Although there are still many solids in the piece, Ann felt at the time that using prints was a daring step that allowed her to stretch her abilities in new ways and create more complex images.

Ann's delightful quilt *Sherlock* captures the flavor of a spring garden. It was a commission for a friend and was made so that two of the borders could be removed and additional blocks added. The quiltmaker wanted the piece to suggest gaiety, humor, springtime, and a positive relationship to nature. Ann says that she particularly likes the effect of latticework within the blocks; it is a design element that she uses often. The diagonal stripe of the sashing and the lines of the quilting help to carry this element throughout the rest of the quilt.

Hearts are the primary motif Ann's quilt *Watching My Children Play*. She used hearts because she made the quilt around St. Valentine's Day. Since Ann wanted the hearts to be prominent, she made them out of brilliant red silks, satins, and metallics. The way in which the design and colors flowed out from the hearts dictated the other fabrics and colors. Ann says, "This quilt really expresses the feelings of pride and joy and love that I have when I can stand back and secretly watch my children play together. Once in a while, they disappoint me, hence the broken heart." This is the first quilt in which Ann used reverse appliqué and fabric painting to introduce a pictorial effect.

Watching My Children Play; *36 by 24 inches; cotton, cotton blends, metallics, and acrylic paint; reverse appliquéd and machine quilted.*

Sherlock; *39 by 26 inches; cotton and cotton blends; machine pieced and machine quilted.*

On a Clear Day You Can See Forever; *42¹/₂ by 66 inches; all-cotton and beads; appliquéd and hand and machine quilted.*

NATASHA KEMPERS-CULLEN

Grids are very important to Natasha Kempers-Cullen's designs. In her quilts a grid can represent a window, doorway, opening, or barrier. A grid is a rigid structure, says Natasha, but it holds possibilities for "breaking the rules" and allows her to be intuitive in the use of color and texture.

Natasha used a grid in her design for *Tourist Trap*, a quilt that incorporates both pictorial and abstract elements. This patchwork quilt depicts many tiny human figures that are walking, running, pointing, and gazing. They are scattered throughout snapshot landscapes made up of brilliant sunset colors. "The tourists are not in any of the landscapes," Natasha says. "They are on the outside, looking in." In this quilt the artist, who uses fiber-reactive dyes in almost all her work, painted five panels that she then cut, rearranged, and pieced into a whole new design. Natasha then sprinkled machine-appliquéd small rectangles over the surface of the quilt. The strong parallel diagonal lines, which she machine quilted, add energy and an offbeat sense of vigor to the theme. Natasha explains that "technically, machine quilting is not easier or faster than hand quilting. This piece took its toll in time, concentration, and a lot of pin-pricked fingers."

On a Clear Day You Can See Forever is an unusual and beguiling quilt. Although it gives the impression of being many separate fabrics pieced together, it is actually a whole-cloth quilt, entirely hand painted with fiber-reactive dyes. Natasha used both machine and hand quilting on this piece and included glass beads as quilting elements in some parts of the quilt. The design, with its metaphysical overtones, was inspired by the artist's work in a sheltered workshop for mentally retarded adults. She found the atmosphere there cheerful and colorful; geraniums filled the sunny windowsills, vivid weavings covered the walls, and the people were warm, friendly, and eager to learn. "This picture just came to me as a result of being there, and I began this piece in one of the workrooms so the clients could see me working," the quiltmaker says.

Natasha says, "Daydreaming stretches my imagination and can provide solutions to creative or technical problems in my work." Her quilt *Daydream at Dusk* started with a doodle that came to symbolize the freedom to daydream, to play, and to develop unique ideas. The design has elements common to all Natasha's work: windows, doorways, and other openings, and the ambiguity of whether the viewer is on the outside looking in or the inside looking out. The quilt is composed of nine small painted panels pieced together, with intense colors flowing around, over, and through each to create a startlingly effective composition. The imagery took shape as the work progressed, and the quiltmaker found it necessary to keep adding panels to fill out the picture. She feels that if she had predetermined the composition, this most likely would have been a whole-cloth quilt.

Tourist Trap; *48 by 64 inches; all-cotton; machine pieced, appliquéd, and machine quilted.*

Daydream at Dusk; *46½ by 28½ inches; all-cotton; machine pieced and hand and machine quilted.*

Stellar Night; *73 by 105 inches; all-cotton;*
machine pieced and hand quilted.

HELEN KING

Fine sewing is second nature to Helen King: She works full time as a needlepoint finisher. For many years she made traditional quilts, following the patterns that everyone uses. "Designing is hard work for me," she says, "execution is easy." But in 1981 Helen began designing her own quilts. Sometimes she starts with a traditional block and then sees how far she can go with it. Her award-winning quilt *Stellar Night* is based on a traditional Windmill block, but instead of using a square quilt block, Helen made a diamond-shaped block and set the diamonds on a point-to-point grid, using sashing to separate them. This change elongates the traditional pattern. "I just take it further than our grandmothers did," the quilter says.

Following a hundred-year-old tradition of making a "freedom quilt" for a boy reaching manhood, Helen made *Stellar Night* for her son's eighteenth birthday. She chose the components of the quilt, including its design, fabric, and stitching pattern, to convey masculinity. The quilter had trouble locating the navy-and-camel-striped fabric, but she refused to settle for another print because she knew the design would not be as effective without it. Now she says, "You can squint your eyes and the stripe helps to set those pieces whirling."

In the prize-winning quilt *Cave Creek Outback*, Helen decided to push the boundaries of a traditional Star pattern. She used a mixture of solid colors and bold, unstructured nontraditional prints because she liked the mottled effect that they gave to the large geometric design of the quilt. She also wanted something that would capture a viewer's attention "from forty feet away," so Helen began to pin fabrics to her design wall until she found the combination that worked best. During the piecing process, she made many changes, but through trial and error, the quiltmaker finally reached the point at which she was happy with the result. The strong straight lines of stitching accentuate the central design and give added power to the quilt, while the color choices call to mind the bright sun and the sere, brown earth of the Sonoran Desert where Helen lives.

When Helen started to work on *Cave Creek 4th of July*, she expected to use many of the same components she had used in *Cave Creek Outback* to capture in cloth the feeling of the town's spectacular holiday fireworks. But this quilt turned out to be difficult in almost every way. At one point Helen became so discouraged that she gave up and did not work on it for seven months—she no longer even liked it. But when Helen finally returned to the quilt, she found that her attitude had changed and the difficulties began to work themselves out; now she is very pleased with this unusual piece. The design explodes out from a central medallion, and the reds, whites, and blues easily evoke the spirit of the Fourth of July.

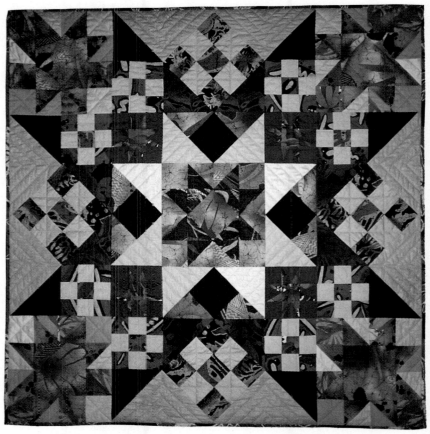

Cave Creek Outback; *47 by 47 inches; cotton and cotton blends; hand quilted.*

Cave Creek 4th of July; *51 by 51 inches; all-cotton; machine pieced and hand quilted.*

La Noche de Rabanos; 53½ by 73 inches; cotton blends, silk, wool, velvet, lamé, braiding, beads, sequins, buttons, and yarn; machine pieced, embroidered, and hand quilted.

ANN KOWALESKI

Ann Kowaleski's quilts are a visual diary of people she has known, places she has been, and events she has celebrated. Some of her quilts have historical themes, some include fantasy, and others blend history and fiction. Ann uses her imagination to express memories and feelings, and she uses color to create a mood and to add rhythm and balance to her quilts. She learned to sew in 4-H, but even though her grandmother was a blue-ribbon quilter, Ann did not make her first quilt until after she had graduated from college. For that quilt she used a traditional Mexican Wedding Cross pattern. Since then, Ann has made about thirty quilts.

Ann's quilt *La Noche de Rabanos* encompasses a variety of quilting techniques, a rich palette of colors, sumptuous fabrics, and many unique embellishments in a shrinelike shape that recalls the carved and painted retablos seen in churches throughout Mexico and the Southwest. The artist, who has spent some time in Mexico, got her inspiration for this award-winning design from a Christmas Eve festival of the same name held in Oaxaca, Mexico. For the fiesta residents grow huge radishes (*rabanos*) and then carve them into figures and scenes that tell stories. The carvings are frequently religious, and the artist used many of these images, including the Christ Child, the Three Kings, and Our Lady of Guadalupe, as well as many kinds of animals, in this piece. Although some parts of the quilt proved difficult because of the fine sewing, braiding, and embroidery required—the figure of Our Lady of Guadalupe was especially challenging—other parts were easy. Ann says that the "shrine" seemed to build itself as soon as she found just the right background color.

The Day of the Dead is also based on Ann's travels in Mexico. The Day of the Dead (November 1) is a major Mexican holiday. "On this day Mexicans flirt with death and add a comic element, yet they take it seriously," Ann says. Processions are held; altars honoring the dead are built and adorned with food, candles, flowers, and personal belongings; and bakery shops and stalls are filled with pastries and sugar candies in the shapes of skeletons, skulls, and lambs. This is a solemn time, but it is also an occasion to rejoice in life. The quiltmaker has captured the inherent flavor and meaning of the day's activities through the almost life-size images on her quilt.

Another one of Ann's quilts, *Her Journal Is Tracks of Bone*, is an ode to the quiltmaker's "large and wonderful black dog of 11 years." Ann spent almost a year working on this quilt—an unusually long time for this artist who often completes her quilts in a few months—because, she says, "I was in the process of mourning." The bones were especially difficult to make. Ann tried various techniques, including painting, but finally settled on reverse appliqué. The quilt is an engaging and fitting tribute to her dog. It is sentimental, but it also sparks an answering and heartfelt emotion in the viewer.

Her Journal Is Tracks of Bone; 86¹/₂ by 96¹/₂ inches; cotton, cotton blends, silk, velvet, beads, and sequins; hand pieced, reverse appliquéd, embroidered, and hand quilted.

The Day of the Dead; 99¹/₂ by 78¹/₂ inches; cotton, cotton blends, silk, wool, velvet, lamé, braiding, beads, sequins, buttons, and horsehair; reverse appliquéd, embroidered, and hand quilted.

Bindas Quilt; *81 by 100 inches; all-cotton; machine pieced and machine quilted.*

JUDITH LARZELERE

When Judith Larzelere decided to make her first quilt, she chose the ambitious Texas Star pattern, hand pieced it with English piecing entirely from scraps she had leftover from other sewing projects, and hand quilted it. After completing this thoroughly traditional first quilt, Judith has always created her own designs. Her early quilts were heavily influenced by her love of Japanese surface designs. Now her abstract designs use flowing lines of color highlighted by glowing pointillist surfaces to project mood and atmosphere. Once she had learned to quilt, Judith quickly developed her own unique and stunning style by experimenting with strip piecing, inspired by the designs of Seminole Indian quilters, and string quilting. "I find designing a long, narrow shape to be challenging," she says. Judith uses machine piecing and quilting to create intricate patterns made up of thousands of small pieces of fabric. Almost all of the one hundred and fifty quilts that she has made have been created with solid-color fabrics, which show the piecing and color interactions to their best advantage.

Even though Judith used Seminole strip piecing and string quilting for *Quilt from Many Ribbons*, its composition, impact, and mood are different from her other quilts. This quilt was inspired by a representative of a ribbon-making company who had seen Judith's quilts and suggested that one made of ribbons would fit both her technique and sense of design. The quiltmaker was intrigued and challenged by the idea, and set to work with about sixty different kinds of ribbon in a variety of soft pastel shades, which reminded her of pale Easter eggs and the fancy dresses worn by small girls. Handling the acetate ribbon turned out to be more difficult than she had anticipated because it tends to crease when it is folded or bent. Judith was nervous when she began to assemble the quilt, but she gained confidence as she progressed and finally completed it to her satisfaction.

The color choices for a quilt representing a sultry summer were easy for Judith: "I see summer as red; I think of the rising heat waves coming off the blacktop streets on an August afternoon." *Red Is for Summer* vividly combines between twenty and thirty brilliant reds, magentas, and oranges, highlighted by darker tones of blue and black. Judith loves working with color and found that the colors in this quilt made it enjoyable to execute.

Judith made *Bindas Quilt* for Jan Bindas, her photographer, in appreciation "for all the wonderful images he has translated onto film for me." The biggest challenge in making this queen-size quilt was to combine a full color spectrum with white while keeping the white patches from visually jumping off the two-dimensional plane. The quilt's design meets this challenge by drawing the viewer's eye into a spiraling kaleidoscope of bright, clear colors dotted with small blocks of white that evoke a mood of activity and excitement but never frenzy.

Quilt from Many Ribbons; *47 by 74 inches; acetate ribbons and brocade; machine pieced and machine quilted.*

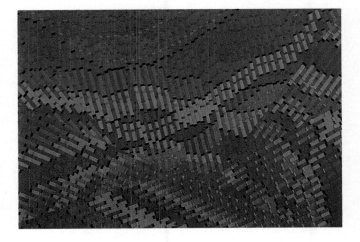

Red Is for Summer; *88 by 42 inches; all-cotton; machine pieced and machine quilted.*

95

Denshoh; *58 by 75¹/₂ inches; all-cotton; machine pieced.*

EMIKO TODA LOEB

Emiko Toda Loeb grew up in Kyoto, Japan, an elegant city where traditional arts and crafts are highly respected. When she moved to the United States, Emiko brought with her the aesthetic sensibilities that are so much a part of Japanese traditions. At the time she was leaving Japan, a new enthusiasm for American patchwork and contemporary quilting was getting underway there. Once she was here, Emiko decided to study American quilts, having enjoyed handwork since her childhood. She is basically a self-taught quilter, but she has attended workshops and sought advice from friends along the way. After several years of study and work, Emiko found that quilting had become much more than the hobby she had intended it to be. Today she teaches patchwork in New York and spends at least several hours a day creating her own quilts. She also returns to Kyoto every summer to visit her parents and teach quilting.

Denshoh is one of the artist's spectacular reversible Log Cabin quilts. Emiko's technique requires the blocks for both sides of the reversible quilt to be assembled simultaneously, with a "log" on one side being attached to its corresponding piece on the other. This method eliminates the need for quilting, but it demands expert skill in design, especially when the two sides are totally different. "If it were only a matter of making one side, the design is very easy," she says, "but when this quilt was made it was still very difficult for me to calculate how the two different sides would work together structurally." Antique kimono fabrics give this piece its richness and depth of color.

Ujō, or "Warmth of Heart," is also a reversible variation on the Log Cabin pattern. The slim bands of small diamond shapes in a mixture of colors sparkle against the deceptively simple two-toned asymmetrical background and highlight the overall simplicity of the design. The cottons, silks, and wools used in this quilt are antique Japanese fabrics. Emiko says, "They seem appropriate to me to use in situations where nothing else is quite right."

Emiko's quilt *Flower Poem* combines many elements to produce a stunning display of lavenders and purples that are thrown into startling relief by a dramatic black background. The quiltmaker used what she calls a "systematic Crazy Quilt" pattern for the colored portion of the quilt. The background is a herringbone pattern made of five different fabrics that give it a varied texture. Emiko used old obis that had been worn with kimonos to funerals, which is the only time that solid black obis are worn. Each of the flowers in the quilt is different, but they are based on similar geometric patterns, and the parts of the flowers are delineated by narrow strips. Emiko says that attaching the narrow strips was the most difficult part of this quilt. Although it is not truly reversible, Emiko put the Manhattan skyline on the back of this quilt.

Ujō; *57 by 75 inches; cotton, silk, and wool; machine pieced.*

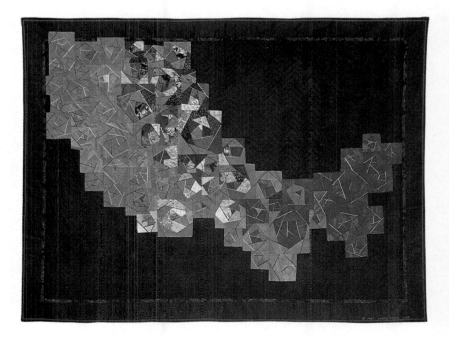

Flower Poem; *91 by 67½ inches; cotton, cotton blends, silk, and rayon; appliquéd and machine pieced.*

Clear Palisades; *92 by 92 inches; all-cotton;
machine pieced and hand quilted.*

LINDA R. MACDONALD

Linda R. MacDonald's oversized quilts are starkly abstract in design, slashed with dramatic diagonals, and cut with windows of vivid color. Her images come from many sources, but nature and art are her primary motivating factors. She became a self-taught quilter after realizing that her style of geometric painting worked admirably when translated to fabric. Linda works mostly with solid-color fabrics, and she paints some areas of her quilts to produce subtle and unusual effects.

The transition from abstract art to quilt design was a natural one for Linda. She sees her quilts as three-dimensional geometric landscapes filled with abstract planes, illusionary objects, and sometimes discordant fields of pattern, which are intended to envelop the viewer with a sense of activity and motion. She overlays her designs with delicate and precise hand stitching that creates a linear latticework and intensifies the energetic imagery created within the body of the quilt.

Linda's quilts are frequently dramatic in scale as well as in concept. She believes that a monumental size gives an artist the opportunity to make a big statement. Her quilt *Titus Canyon* measures a majestic 10 by 11 feet. Linda spent nearly a year making this quilt and the size, which is large even by her standards, gave Linda several unexpected problems. She had to build a large extension for her quilting frame, but the extra length made the whole piece sag. Once she had solved the technical problems, Linda was able to concentrate on the design, which is made up of pieced and appliquéd images. The title of the quilt refers to a canyon in Death Valley that contains many of the same subtle colors as Linda's hand-dyed fabrics. The design gives the illusion of geometric progressions presented on a patterned plane with color, organization, and pattern working together to create an environment.

In *Clear Palisades* Linda has achieved a stunning effect through the juxtaposition of strong elements. The bars and planes that form the major image seem to twist and change as they move through the quilt. Some areas of the quilt have depth and dimension, while others remain flat. The entire quilt is pieced, but there are no traditional blocks. Each section carries its own sense of identity and power, and the intriguing color shifts, achieved through a combination of hand-dyed and commercial fabrics, highlight the drama of the design. Linda added patches of brighter blue to the quilt during its production because she felt that an area along the horizon line did not hold up when she used only the colors she had originally planned. Even though this quilt was machine pieced, the artist hand quilted it with a profusion of elaborate designs. The extra dimension added by the quilting is particularly visible on the reverse side of the quilt, which also carries a simple geometric pieced design. Linda says that a large undecorated quilt back "makes me want to fill it up."

Titus Canyon; *120 by 132 inches; all-cotton; machine and hand pieced, appliquéd, and hand quilted.*

Clear Palisades *(detail).*

Reflections II: On Autumn; *70 by 70 inches;
all-cotton and lamé; machine pieced and machine
quilted.*

JAN MAHER

Jan Maher made her first quilt—an original design of sailboats stuffed and appliquéd to a background of heavy black satin—because she needed a bed cover, but it ended up hanging on the wall instead. Jan has been doing needlework since she was a child and considers herself to be a self-taught quilter. The inspiration for her quilts comes primarily from three sources—nature, her own experiences, and political issues. She expresses these themes through designs that deal with space, contrasts, and ambiguities as they relate to the formal visual elements as well as human emotions.

Jan's quilt *Reflections I* was a difficult quilt for her to make. Its construction was like industrial R & D (research and development) for a new product, she says. "The most difficult part was trying to translate color from small-scale studies into fabric on a much larger scale." In making the quilt, Jan worked from a scale drawing and relied on measurements for cutting the pieces. She used strip piecing in some areas and employed the fast-piecing technique for the bands of triangles. The design of this quilt is based on architectural imagery: The viewer is inside a building, looking out through its windows into the windows of a neighboring building. With her choice of fabric pattern and composition, Jan created strong vertical and horizontal lines that accentuate the structural sense and enhance the impression of visually entering other space. For the artist this quilt brings back memories of living and working in high-rise buildings in downtown Chicago.

The second quilt in her Reflections series, *Reflections II: On Autumn*, is based on the major design elements of *Reflections I*. Jan says that it "looks out the windows of my present home in North Carolina into a forest of fall colors on a beautiful autumn day. The quilt is not loaded with symbolism; it is an impression of one face of nature." Jan again worked from a scale drawing, but instead of doing color studies on paper, she coordinated all the colors with full-size pieces of fabric on her work wall. This quilt is strip pieced, and Jan says that the most difficult part was trying to keep the long, narrow strips of fabric straight and flat while she sewed. Most of the fabric in this quilt, as in all her quilts, is made of natural fibers because, she says, "I cannot stand the smell of polyester when it is ironed!"

Reflections III: Atypical Spring also plays off the design elements in the other Reflections quilts, but it gets additional inspiration from Frank Lloyd Wright's art-glass windows and creates a luminous and complex composition of color and design. The larger solid areas are integrated into the design through intricate stitched patterns, adding yet another level of complexity. Jan feels that this quilt was in some ways an exercise in ambivalence. "To this day," she says, "I am not sure whether I like it or not. I got discouraged at many points, but when I look back, I think that it ended up being one of my more powerful pieces."

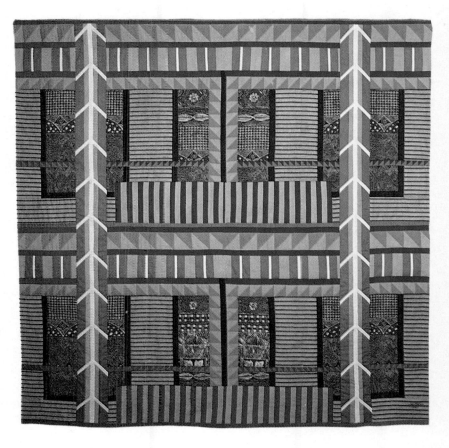

Reflections I; *70 by 69 inches; all-cotton; machine pieced and machine quilted.*

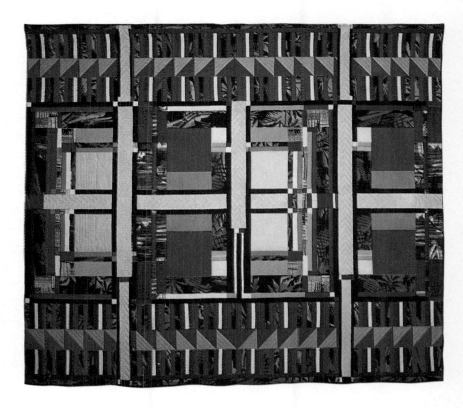

Reflections III: Atypical Spring; *84 1/2 by 72 inches; all-cotton; machine pieced and hand and machine quilted.*

Desert Sunrise; *42 by 53 inches; cotton, cotton blends, silk, linen, satin, flannel, and beads; machine and hand pieced, appliquéd, and machine and hand quilted.*

MARGUERITE MALWITZ

Marguerite Malwitz never expected that she would one day be a quilter rather than a weaver. She had been interested in weaving, batik, tie-dye, and fabric printing for as long as she can remember, and for fifteen years she worked as a weaver and assistant to Ina Golub who designs tapestries. "In those years," she says, "I perfected my by-hand techniques and grew to love color and fabric." But she credits her skill at sewing to a junior high teacher.

Marguerite now makes quilted fabric "paintings" of her direct experiences in nature. The seashores of the East Coast and deserts of the Southwest are two of her favorite themes. Marguerite says that these places present refreshingly different design elements and color combinations. She finds the contrast helpful when she needs a change in her work. To create her engaging collages, Marguerite may include found objects, such as shells or driftwood; soft appliqués; heavily textured fabrics; stamped images; or heavy stitchery.

Desert Sunrise is a quilt filled with glowing color. A walk through the Desert Botanical Gardens in Phoenix, Arizona, inspired Marguerite to make this quilt, in which five different kinds of cacti are represented. The quilting lines suggest the natural ridges in cactus plants. Small brightly colored silk scraps form the flowers, and beads and embroidery thread create the stickers on the prickly pear cactus in the foreground. The artist says she had not planned to make a sunrise scene, but it turned out that the oranges and lavenders of a desert dawn worked best with the other colors in the quilt.

Martha's Vineyard: Three Yellow Umbrellas is part of a series that pictures the beach, sea, umbrellas, and sea grass. Marguerite decided not to use a block format for this quilt, feeling that it would interrupt the panorama of the scene. She used strip piecing to create the effect of waving sea grass, choosing the colors and fabrics for the grass first and then deciding on the rest of the materials in the quilt. Metallic thread gives the impression of foam and light reflecting from the water's surface. Marguerite attached shells to buttons using a hot melting process and then sewed them to the quilt, so that they litter a dune path leading down to the sea.

In *Undersea Scallops* Marguerite created a large shell with strip piecing and then set it in a pieced background. This quilt is part of a series of five quilts that uses different combinations of the same templates with different fabrics. Some of the fabric in this piece is a silk-screen print made by an artist in the Caribbean. Marguerite says that friends often bring her fabrics from their travels because "they know I love fabrics with printed textures that remind me of land- and seascapes." The underwater feeling created by this charming quilt is enhanced by attached sea shells, hand-stamped sea shells, and free-form machine quilting that suggests the rippling of water over the bottom of the sea.

Undersea Scallops; *16 by 12 inches; cotton, cotton blends, silk, metallic thread, and sea shells; machine pieced, appliquéd, and machine and hand quilted. Collection of Kathryn Chambers Turcotte.*

Martha's Vineyard: Three Yellow Umbrellas; *48 by 25 inches; cotton, cotton blends, silk, metallic thread, and sea shells; machine and hand pieced, appliquéd, and hand quilted.*

103

Tornado III; *52¹⁄₄ by 64¹⁄₂ inches; cotton, silk,
polyester organza, laser copy heat-transferred to
fabric, and buttons; machine pieced and machine
bar tacked.*

MERRILL MASON

Merrill's three Tornado quilts form a graphic and powerful series in which tornado imagery is a metaphor for physical and emotional turmoil. For the artist the issue is order versus chaos, especially the tension between trying to maintain control and losing control. The photographs used in *Tornado I* are meant to capture a sense of the vulnerability that a storm can leave in its wake. The artist says, "I've always been struck by photographs showing the aftermath of a tornado, where houses are ripped open and the most personal objects of a life, mingled with the mundane, are strewn at random for the public to see" The swirling patterns coming out of the photos represent wind currents, and the appliqués and found objects sewn over the quilt represent the artifacts strewn about by the tornado.

In *Tornado I* the mood is dark and somber, but not without optimism. The stunning background is airbrushed and hand painted. After she painted it, Merrill ripped it into strips and then reassembled it. The back of the quilt is also hand painted, then sewn with guinea hen feathers and overlaid with transparent, iridescent organza.

Tornado III also makes highly effective use of both sides of the quilt. The front, composed of painted organza blocks sewn to a painted cotton square, is ablaze with color. The border has a stamped text of an eyewitness account by a man who was "run over by a tornado and lived to tell his tale." The back, with its heat-transferred and hand-colored laser print, continues the text, but it is almost peaceful by comparison to the fiery front. The tornado image is buttoned on rather than stitched down to the back. Merrill felt that the quilt design did not work as long as she was trying to put the tornado on the front, but it fell into place once she made the decision to use both sides.

To make *Postcard Quilt*, Merrill photocopied images and colored them with dye sticks and then added hand stamping. Even though the block design is fairly simple, printing the fabric was a slow process and there were times when the artist felt distinctly bogged down with the stamping. But her excitement with the finished squares kept her going.

Buttons and Fortunes is a whimsical quilt that is made up of the colors Merrill likes best, warm and glowing pinks, peaches, and golds, and things that she likes to collect, from buttons to Chinese cookie fortunes. She photocopied the fortunes, which range from the sublime ("You will be fortunate in everything you put your hands to.") to the ridiculous ("You may attend a party where strange customs prevail."), and transferred them onto cotton fabric. Merrill then placed the fortunes in loose tulle bags that hold them in place but allow the fortunes to be read. Hand-printed triangles add an extra dimension to the quilt as their bottom points curl away and cast shadows against the background. There is no real quilting in this piece; instead, the hand-sewn buttons act as ties.

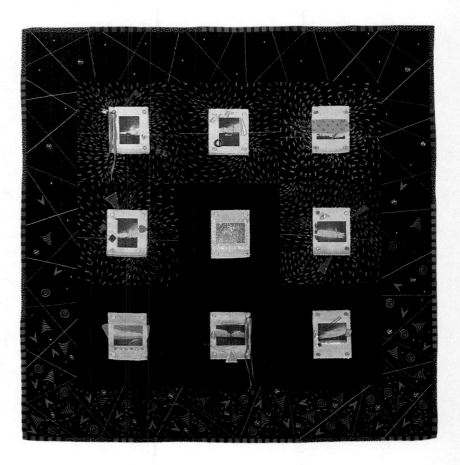

Tornado I; 49 by 48½ inches; cotton, cotton blends, color copy heat-transferred to fabric, metallic thread, buttons, beads, and found objects; machine pieced, machine embroidered, and machine bar tacked.

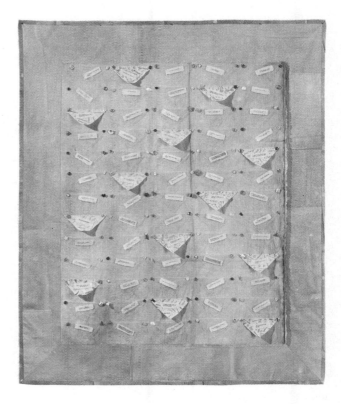

Buttons and Fortunes; 45½ by 54 inches; cotton, polyester tulle, color copy heat-transferred to fabric, buttons, and metallic thread; machine pieced and hand tied with buttons.

MERRILL MASON

Tornado II; *40 by 56 inches; cotton, polyester*
organza, metallic thread, color copy
heat-transferred to fabric, and feathers; machine
pieced and machine bar tacked.

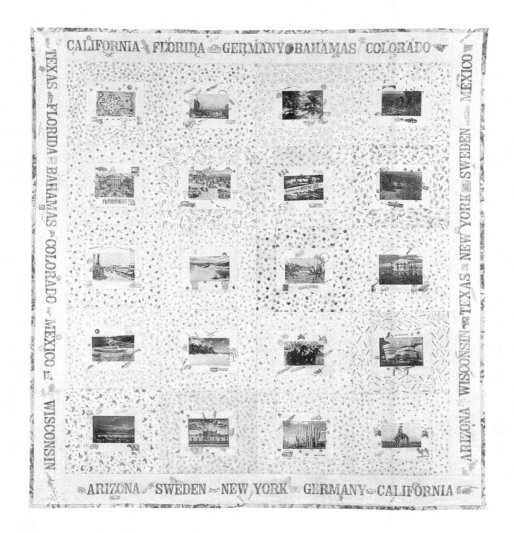

Postcard Quilt; *63 by 67 inches; all-cotton with color copy heat-transferred to fabric; machine pieced and machine quilted with trapunto.*

Postcard Quilt *(detail).*

Postcard Quilt *(detail).*

Friendship Fan; *25 by 30 inches; all-cotton;
machine and hand pieced, and hand quilted.*

JUDY MATHIESON

Judy Mathieson made her first quilt to complete her undergraduate degree in home economics. Faced with a project that called for a combination of tie-dyed, printed, and batik fabrics, she decided that the only answer was to work them all into a quilt. One quilt led to another, and before long she found herself a full-time quiltmaker who was teaching quilting, publishing patterns, and judging competitions rather than teaching high school home economics. She has now made more than fifty quilts of many sizes.

Judy draws inspiration for her quilts from such diverse sources as antique quilt patterns, her husband's woodworking books, wallpaper designs, and windows. She prefers to work with a pattern or shape that people recognize easily and creates new designs as well as variations of traditional patterns, such as Fan, Mariner's Compass, Tumbling Blocks, and Attic Window. "Complex designs intrigue me," she says. She likes to use color and fabric to create a three-dimensional effect in her work.

The pattern for Judy's quilt *Nautical Stars* began with a Compass Rose watercolor painted by an unknown sailor in the early 1800s. Pennsylvania Dutch hex signs and compass motifs seen on old nautical charts and quilts inspired the designs for the twinkling abundance of stars scattered over the quilt. The huge, multicolored central star, with its subtle gradations of tone and surrounding aureole of rings composed of tiny triangles, seems to spin, and the smaller stars appear to burst out of the shaded background of an enchanted sky. The quilting, which radiates from the central design, accentuates a sense of the unconfined energy and beauty of the universe. The biggest problem with this piece was keeping track of all the small pieces of fabric and seeing that they reached their proper places.

Friendship Fan is a delightful display of friendship and design. The artist picked the pattern, which is based on a 1930s Fan quilt, and the background fabrics from leftover pieces of *Nautical Stars*, and then each member of her quilt group made a block. Judy assembled the blocks when they were complete and did the quilting. The four plain blocks with quilted fans represent friends who could no longer participate in the group. The final product is a wonderful medley of color and pattern working together in harmony—just like the group.

For *Plaid Compass Rose*, Judy took a favorite design and combined it with many of her favorite elements from antique Compass quilts, including blocks on points, the use of many fabrics, cutout roses applied with a blanket stitch, appliqué in the triangular border blocks, and over-and-under sashing. A plaid quilting design complements the overall pattern, while a complex use of fabric and color adds sparkle and verve to the Compass blocks.

Plaid Compass Rose; *96 by 96 inches; all-cotton; hand pieced and machine quilted.*

Nautical Stars; *73 by 88 inches; all-cotton; machine pieced and hand quilted.*

Upside Down Cupcake; *84 by 84 inches; various fabrics and acrylic paint; machine appliquéd and hand tied.*

THERESE MAY

Therese May believes in free expression in art, whatever the medium. "Art is one of the few things we have in this world where we can say or do almost anything we want." This artist's brightly colored and seemingly chaotic quilts, vibrating with energy, are lively statements of the things she wants to say about the world. Therese used to be a painter, but she switched to quiltmaking shortly after the birth of her first child, when she realized that painting and caring for a young child were not always compatible.

Therese has devised her own methods for working with fabric, and most of her quilts follow the same construction format. She starts with a drawing and uses it to cut the fabric pieces. Then she pins the pieces to a muslin backing and machine appliqués them in place. She does not cut loose threads but lets them float free to form a network of texture over the surface of the quilt. When the quilt is completed, Therese paints it. "I like the element of risk involved with finishing a quilt that takes weeks or months to do and then painting on it with the possibility of ruining it." Therese used to make geometric patterns, but she now uses fairly realistic photographic images in her work, much of which is based on intuitive fantasy imagery with animals, plants, and scenes of hearth and home. *Sugar Bowl*, for example, is a delightful quilt that radiates energy. The homeyness of the bowl is offset by the fanciful animals that swim, fly, and cavort around it.

Upside Down Cupcake takes a childhood remembrance and turns it into an imaginary birthday cake. The artist says, "In Madison, Wisconsin, where I grew up, there is a water reservoir shaped like a giant upside down cupcake. It was all covered with grass, and my friends and I used to climb it and run around on top of it. In this quilt I'm just having a little fun with the idea." The wide border of the quilt is like a highly decorated picture frame for the central image. Her bright and cheerful quilt *Apple Cookie Jar* also conjures up a happy hodgepodge of childhood memories.

Therese's quilt *Rose* is a softly blooming symbol of gratitude, love, appreciation, and peace. Two frivolous and imaginative little fish seem to be paying homage to the flower as it rests in solitary glory against a lattice of pretty prints and colors. *Basket* is another colorful compilation of childhood dreams and fantasies. It symbolizes a safe place to be, with all the little creatures inside well protected from the snakes and monsters without.

Cup is "a kind of personal symbol for oneness," says the artist. The pattern surrounding the cup represents a braided rug, made of many little pieces that create a whole. To Therese the braided rug evokes a feeling of America's past and a sense of hearth and home; it is an element that she frequently uses in her work. The many little amoebalike fish painted around the border seem to be swimming through the interior frame to reach the cup.

Sugar Bowl; *84 by 84 inches; various fabrics and acrylic paint; machine appliquéd and hand tied.*

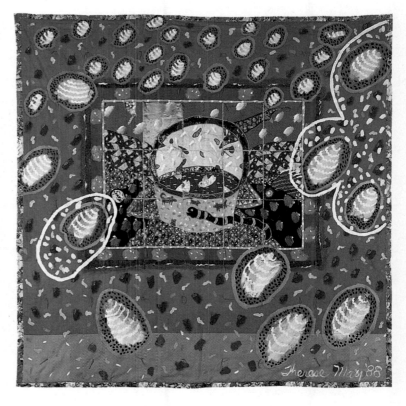

Basket; *84 by 84 inches; various fabrics and acrylic paint; machine appliquéd and hand tied.*

111

Apple Cookie Jar; *84 by 84 inches; various*
fabrics and acrylic paint; machine appliquéd and
hand tied.

JUDITH MONTAÑO

Judith Montaño is a former painter who now makes Crazy Quilts because she believes that they are the most painterly of all quilts. In much the same way that a painter lays down paint layer by layer to build up a surface, a crazy quilter lays down pieces of fabric, lace, ribbon, and other adornments, carefully choosing each with design and impact in mind, to create shimmering, enticing compositions. Judith's great-grandmother was a master quilter, but in addition to growing up with quilts, this artist, who is a native of Canada, feels that her own work has been influenced by living in England, Germany, and Japan, and spending her childhood on a cattle ranch next to an Indian reservation. Judith started quilting in 1976 while she was living in Texas. In 1980 she had the honor of winning best of show at the Calgary Exhibition and Stampede in Calgary, Alberta. Her great-grandmother had won the same award in 1934.

Judith gave *Crazy Quilts Then and Now* a Victorian flavor by using antique fabrics and pictorial cigarette silks but she brings the quilt up to date with a center block that depicts a Southwestern landscape. The quilt is a joyful collage of antique and modern techniques and materials, including appliqué, hand-dyed fabrics, embroidery, beading, ribbon work, painting on velvet, calligraphy, and photography. It affirms the reason that this artist is so enamored of the process: "Crazy quilting satisfies a lot of needs and has few rules," she says. "It lets you be the artist."

Crazy Quilt Friends is another delightful collage; it has a special meaning to the artist. When she moved from Texas to Colorado, the members of her quilt group each made a Crazy Quilt piece for her as a surprise going-away present. Each of the 40 pieces has the name or initials of its maker. The group presented them to Judith pinned to a piece of muslin, along with instructions to please finish the quilt in time for the guild's next quilt show. The artist added her own unique pieces and embellishments, and everyone was delighted when it won a judge's choice award at the state fair. As was common with Crazy Quilts of earlier years, this one is a repository of happy memories.

Judith is exceptionally busy: She works part time as a staff aide in the textile department of the Denver Art Museum, where she helps to document and catalogue an extensive quilt collection. She teaches three times a year in Japan, where the Crazy Quilt technique is especially popular, and once a year she does an Australian tour, traveling throughout the country to give lectures and workshops. She has published two books and made a video on Crazy Quilt techniques, and her designs have been featured in many magazines and other publications. With all these activities, she still finds time to create new quilts, always trying to push crazy quilting just one step further. "The beauty of it all," she says, "is that I'm doing what I love."

Crazy Quilt Friends; *60 by 60 inches; silk, velvet, cotton, metallic thread, lace, buttons, ribbons, and other embellishments; machine and hand pieced, embroidered, and appliquéd.*

Crazy Quilt Friends *(detail).*

The French Bouquet Variation; *79 by 94 inches; all-cotton; hand appliquéd and hand quilted with trapunto.*

JOANNE F. MOULDEN

When Joanne F. Moulden was growing up, a quilting frame was always set up and in use in her home. Both her mother and her grandmother were quilters, but even though she has painted, made ceramics, and done all kinds of needlework, Joanne did not begin quilting until she gave up her nursing career. "I knew I would really enjoy quilting," she says, "but I also really didn't know much about it." Joanne had learned basic sewing skills as a child, but she had to learn many quilting techniques on her own or in workshops.

An exhibit of special heirloom quilts that she had once seen in Washington, D.C., inspired Joanne to make *The French Bouquet Variation*. She wanted to make a quilt that matched the beauty and technique of these quilts. Joanne's quilt is a breathtaking floral display made up of padded and embroidered pastel blooms, tied with bows and framed by two sizes of trailing vine-and-leaf borders. The quiltmaker's use of trapunto gives depth and richness to the quilt, just as the luxuriant mass of flowers at the quilt's top accentuates the delicacy of the smaller bouquets. Joanne quilted feather wreaths with center stippling between the bouquets, while diagonal stitching forms an overall background. Quilted plumed feathers wind their way around the border, with crosshatching behind. Joanne made this quilt during a long illness when she felt that she needed a project that would provide a challenge. The quilt represents a great achievement to the artist; it saw her through a difficult period in which she suffered a lot of pain.

The Berkeley Springs Quilt is an original design made in honor of the artist's hometown. She chose the colors to reflect the scenery of the area. Within each of its four large blocks, a central blue square represents the hot springs for which the town is famous, the small muslin triangles are the bath house, and the larger multicolor print square is the park. Other elements in the quilt represent the nearby towns and the surrounding mountains, and the borders carry through the same elements. The magnificent and precise quilting has original feather plumes in each corner backed by stippling, and each sawtooth triangle is outlined with straight-line stitching. Echo quilting outlines the sawtooth mountains.

Joanne used to be the director for a regional quilters' association, developing new groups and running workshops to increase interest in the craft. Now she teaches classes of eight students in her own studio three days a week from September through May and expects each student to complete a full- or queensize bed quilt during the school year. In addition to quilting skills, the students also learn about drafting and design. Joanne says that "teaching is very rewarding. The talent is definitely out there." When she is not teaching, preparing for classes, or traveling to give workshops, Joanne spends five to ten hours a day on her own quilting projects. "After all, I have to stay ahead of my students," she says.

The Berkeley Springs Quilt; *80 by 80 inches; all-cotton; hand pieced and hand quilted.*

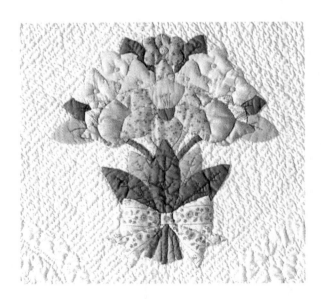

The French Bouquet Variation *(detail)*.

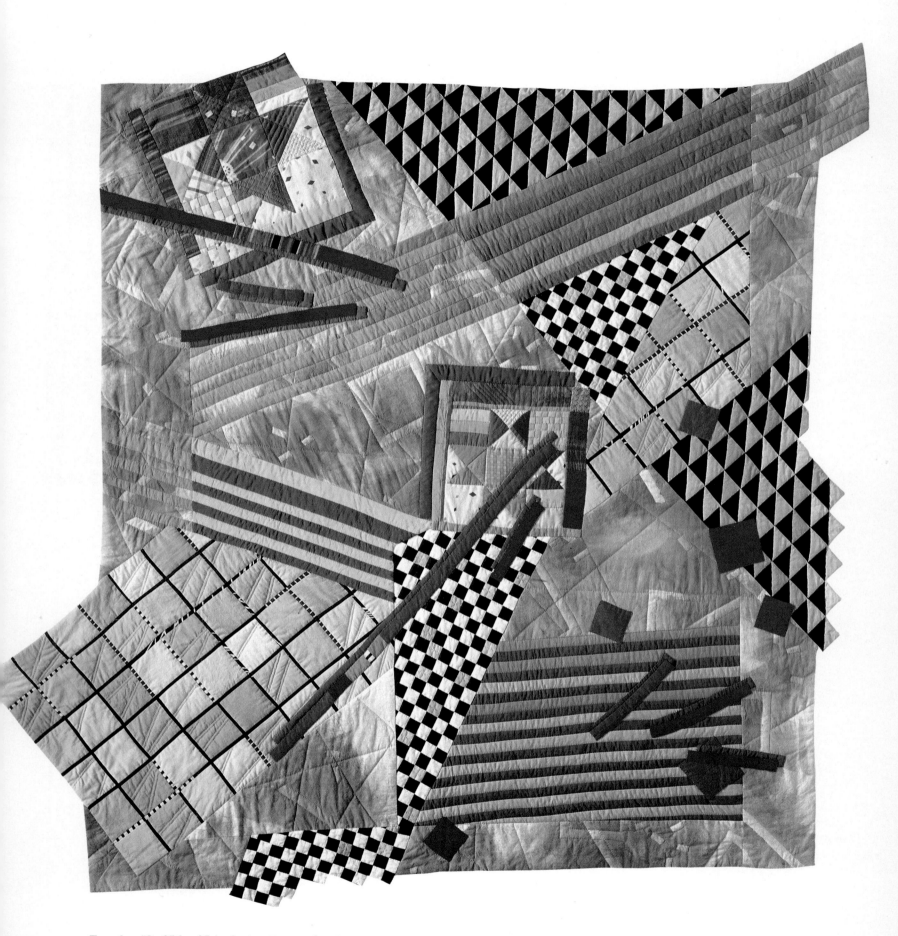

Travelog #2; 65 by 65 inches; cotton and cotton
blends; machine pieced, appliquéd, and hand
quilted.

CLARE M. MURRAY

Clare M. Murray considers herself a professional quiltmaker. "I work at my profession six to eight hours a day," she says. "But I have the best of all worlds—my job and my hobby are the same." She makes between six and ten quilts every year, often working on two at time. Clare learned the basics of sewing from her mother, and she has taken classes from many well-known quilters. Clare's first quilts were traditional, but now she develops her own designs. "I think of myself as an artist, only I work with fabric instead of paint," she says of her provocative, asymmetrical quilts that explore architectural elements—windows, arches, doorways, and stairs—and their relationship to space.

Clare often works in series, developing several quilts that are related in concept and use similar design elements expressed in many different ways. "A series allows me to do more than one interpretation," she says. Her quilt *Artificial Environment #1*, the first in a series depicts architectural elements in what she calls "not so real" atmospheres. Windows, arches, and stairs are suspended in space, leading nowhere and everywhere; sharp angles and soft curves are juxtaposed in tantalizing and unexpected ways. The quilt makes use of individual templates or pattern pieces that are often used only once, a hallmark of the artist's method of design. Also typical of Clare's work is the absence of straight borders. Her designs seem to contain too much energy to be held within traditional constraints, and elements that jump beyond a quilt's confines are not unusual.

Clare's Travelog series translates into fabric the Old World architectural shapes and forms of which she became so fond during a six-month sojourn in Europe. *Travelog #2*, a brilliant award-winning quilt, was inspired by two seemingly incongruous elements: roughly patterned cobblestone streets and the wide open sky. Bold checkerboard patterns appear to float across a delicately hued hand-dyed and hand-painted background representing the sky. The pattern of the quilting is a reflection of the geometry of the streets, while the irregular shape of the quilt allows the elements a sense of freedom that enhances the overall concept. This quilt includes a traditional Ohio Star quilt block because the artist had the urge "to do something traditional in an innovative way."

Strong images of long, narrow alleys and hidden courtyards in southern Europe are evoked by *Travelog #3*, a quilt that Clare says was "a challenge from beginning to end." It is composed of two large blocks that are mirror images, but they are hard to distinguish because of various exceptions to the regular quilt piecing. Because the elements do not fit together in a traditional block-to-block fashion, this quilt was a monumental construction task that required creative piecing and hand appliqué. The finished quilt achieves Clare's goal of depicting a sensation of depth and the enigmatic transparency of space.

Travelog #3; *100 by 76 inches; cotton and cotton blends; machine pieced hand and machine appliquéd, and hand quilted.*

Artificial Environment #1 *62 by 65 inches; cotton and cotton blends; machine pieced, appliquéd, and hand quilted.*

Precipice; *75 by 93 inches; all-cotton; machine
pieced and machine quilted.*

JAN MYERS-NEWBURY

Hand-dyed fabrics are integral to Jan Myers-Newbury's quilts. She started working with pieced fabrics while she was studying design in graduate school. The medium gave her a way to execute color and design problems on a large scale. For a while Jan did not realize that her fabric pieces could become quilts, and when she first started to quilt, her technique was "improper," she says; she used five-eighths-inch seams, for example. But Jan eventually learned all the "proper" methods through books, picking up tips from other quilters, and her own experiences. Her work continues to deal with color and design problems, which she enjoys the challenge of solving. But her color choices are often influenced by sights she has seen, the season, a painting, or almost anything exciting or interesting.

Precipice shows the artist's fabric dyeing skills to great advantage. She had been using tie-dyeing techniques for several years, but this is the first quilt for which Jan tied the fabric in a specific pattern before dyeing it. The resulting diagonal pattern, which is pieced to fragment the pattern slightly, was the starting point for the rest of the quilt's design that highlights this diagonal element. To the artist the quilt represents a spiritual journey: "The simplicity of the design is a reaction to the direction my work has been taking; the symmetry feels centered," she says. She also sees duality in the piece: "There is the obvious contrast between hot and cold colors, but also a sense of heaven and hell, even though the composition has a clear upward thrust."

The Gardens at Giverny captures the impressionistic rush of vivid colors always associated with Monet's spectacular gardens. The use of the lime green was inspired by an Impressionist painting that the artist had seen, but she does not remember who painted it. Traditional Crazy Quilts provided another source of inspiration for the work. "I love doing these Crazy Quilts," Jan says. "They give me a format for experimenting with color—by fragmenting it to such a degree, almost anything is acceptable." The palette of tie-dyed fabrics is consistent throughout the surface of this quilt, while the solid colors shift from light values at the center to darker ones on the perimeter. The border is composed entirely of tie-dyed pieces. An overlaid lattice pattern brings order to the design and relates back to the flower garden theme.

Red Light Green Light is one quilt in a series that explores color interaction on a grid format. Jan used to make quilts composed only of squares and rectangles, and she designed this piece during that period although she constructed it more recently. "I don't know why I never made that quilt," she says, "because it was a good drawing. I guess it was just waiting for me to start using tie-dyed fabric." Jan believes that many of her earlier quilts led up to this one and that in many ways it demonstrates the fact that the simplest design is often the most effective.

The Gardens at Giverny; *58 by 48 inches; all-cotton; machine pieced and machine quilted.*

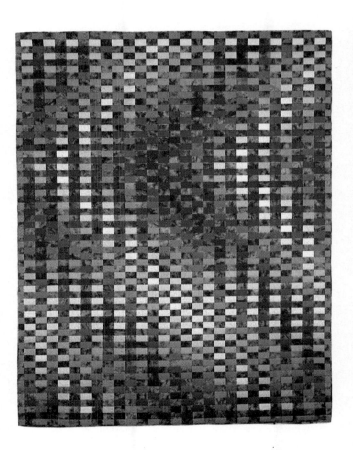

Red Light Green Light; *72 by 96 inches; all-cotton; machine pieced and machine quilted.*

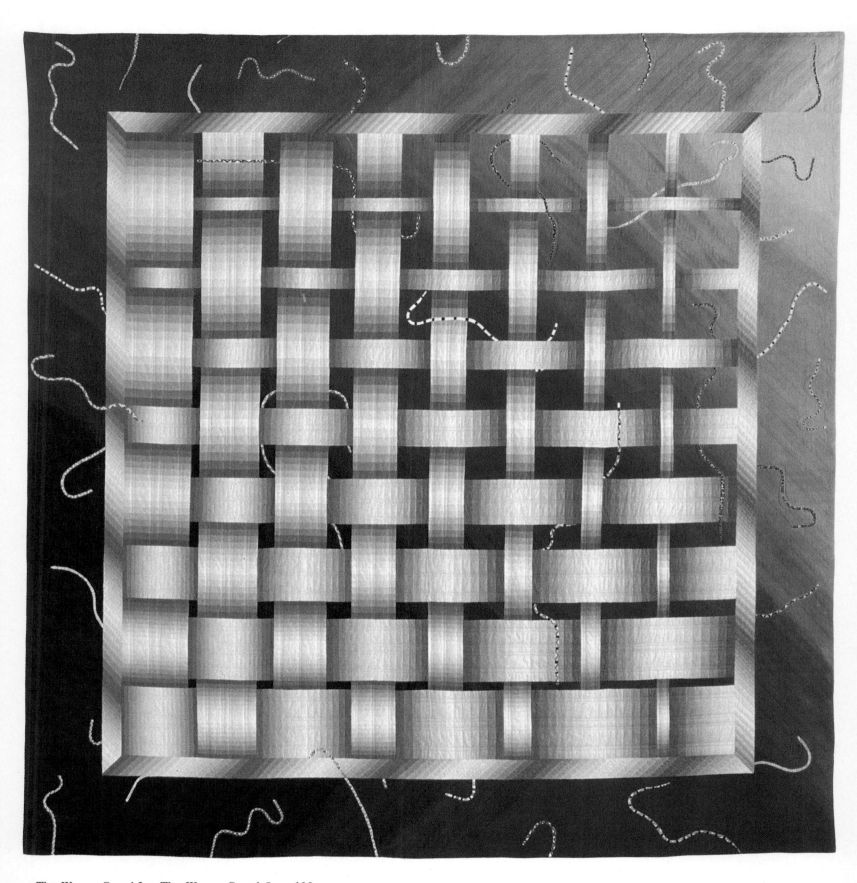

The Worms Crawl In—The Worms Crawl Out; *100 by 100 inches; all-cotton; machine pieced, appliquéd, and hand quilted.*

MIRIAM NATHAN-ROBERTS

Miriam Nathan-Roberts says that her quilts deal with illusions of depth. "I had no depth perception until I was thirty years old, so I like creating illusions of depth on a two-dimensional surface." Even though she studied clothing and design in college, Miriam says her first quilt, which she started in 1972, was a disaster, so she decided to take quilt-making classes. After that there was no turning back. "This is not a passing hobby—I treat it seriously," she says. After making a few traditional quilts, Miriam started creating her own designs. She likes to work in series and now has two in progress: an Interweave series and an Architecture series.

Her quilt *The Worms Crawl In—The Worms Crawl Out* is a study in contrasts. The rigid lattice of its interwoven grid is a perfect foil for randomly placed, loosely flowing hand-painted worm shapes that wind sinuously in, out, and over the structural elements. The soft tones of the background contrast with the hard, metallic look of the grid. Neither the design nor its execution was easy. The background is hand dyed, and it took several tries to get the desired ombré effect. The appliquéd grid shifts in tone from dark to light and back to dark in every segment, each of which is composed of narrow strips. Since every row is different, the sizes of the graduating strips change continuously. "Putting it together was very confusing," Miriam says. She hand quilted this piece under the direction of Sarah Henderson.

Only three of the boxes in *Nancy's Fancy* are actually complete; the others seem to lose their sides as they explode away from the center. "The piece started out to be serious," says Miriam. "But when I put the polka dots behind the boxes, thinking they would act as a grid, they took over and the piece immediately became more whimsical and more fun." Even though the piecing of this quilt was difficult, worse was the fact that "most of my friends thought that I had lost my mind," reminisces the artist. "They were not prepared for the use of such bold fabrics at that time." The work gets its name from Miriam's friend Nancy Halpern, who encouraged her to use wildly patterned material.

The Museum, which joins pictorial and abstract design, was inspired by the Museum of Contemporary Art in Los Angeles. The design developed as the quilt was constructed. The blocks represent rooms of paintings in the museum, and the brilliant fabric patterns give the impression of modern art. The figures are people visiting the museum, and the small seated figure with a telephone is the ticket taker at the museum's entrance. This composition seems to float in space, and overall, there is a sense of airiness, light and excitement about art. The strong diagonals of the quilting help enhance the feeling that you are involved in a new and thrilling experience.

Miriam holds a master's degree in educational psychology and teaches special education half time. She works in her quilting studio as much as possible.

The Museum; *58 by 63 inches; cotton and cotton blends; machine pieced and hand quilted.*

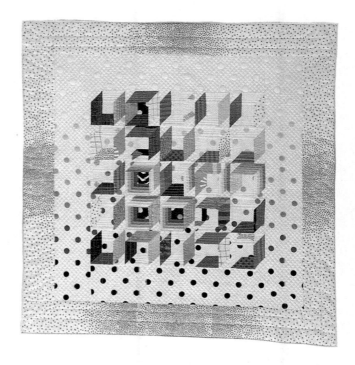

Nancy's Fancy; *54 by 54 inches; cotton and cotton blends; machine pieced and hand quilted.*

Mayflower; *79 by 95 inches; cotton and cotton blends; machine pieced and hand quilted.*

JULIA OVERTON NEEDHAM

Julia Overton Needham started her first quilt, *Trip Around the World*, during a school vacation when she was a teenager. "But then it was put away, unfinished and forgotten for 35 years." Finding it again and completing it inspired Julia to keep on quilting.

Julia bases her original designs on traditional block patterns, which she alters to create new and interesting designs. She occasionally purchases new material specifically for a quilt, but mostly Julia works with fabrics already in her collection of cottons and cotton blends. Her mother gave her a small selection of fabrics but Julia has bought the rest of her collection mostly on a whim. Julia tries to include some of the pieces she received from her mother in each of her quilts because they bring back warm memories of her mother and her childhood.

Bridal Stairway is a good example of the way in which this quilter works. Julia had seen a Bridal Stairway block in a quilting book and found it appealing. But she thought that an entire quilt built of the block would be boring and decided to leave space between the blocks; this provided an ideal spot for a simple appliqué. She designed a symmetrical pattern of flowers and leaves that enhanced the beauty of the traditional block and added a new dimension. Julia says that coming up with the right design for this quilt was the hardest part in its development, but selecting the right colors was a close second because she wanted to purchase as little material as possible. The lavender she used for the background was ultimately her only purchase.

For her quilt *Lavender Blue*, Julia designed appliquéd blocks that are set together with traditional Garden Maze sashing. The appliquéd pattern draws the viewer's eye from corner to corner in an X pattern that corresponds to the X formed by the sashing. The patterned fabric enclosed by the Garden Maze serves to emphasize the linear sense of this piece, and the artist has carried the relation between the elements even further by her choice of a border fabric that repeats a portion of the print enclosed within the maze. Even though this design looks simple, Julia found it exceptionally difficult to develop. Initially she had no confidence that the quilt had merit, but her reservations were dispelled when it won three awards.

The quilter says that *Mayflower* really kept her on her toes. The quilt uses one basic block that is repeated and placed together edge to edge. The design is formed by the manipulation of color within each block. Keeping all the pieces in the proper place while she machine pieced them required Julia's constant concentration. The hand quilting forms flowing rosettes that are shown to their best advantage in the areas of solid color. She also gave herself an additional challenge in the creation of this quilt by deciding to use only fabrics that she had on hand.

Lavender Blue; *72 by 90 inches; cotton and cotton blends; hand pieced, appliquéd, and hand quilted.*

Bridal Stairway; *100 by 79 inches; cotton and cotton blends; hand pieced, appliquéd, and hand quilted.*

Iris; *84 by 102 inches; all-cotton; appliquéd and hand quilted.*

VELDA E. NEWMAN

Hydrangea; *99 by 84 inches; all-cotton; appliquéd and hand quilted.*

Once Velda E. Newman found that she could combine her interest in art with her skill at sewing to make quilts of her own design, she found that everything around her seemed to stimulate new ideas for quilts. But for her nature and color usually play a large part in shaping the final images. She considers color the most important element in developing a design; "that's what draws attention," she says. When Velda began work on a new project recently, she envisioned rich purples and tawny golds, and then realized that a composition of fruit, such as grapes and pears, would be ideal for the colors she had in mind.

The size of the quilt is another important factor in Velda's designs. Large quilts are a problem because they take such a long time to make and there is so much of them to work with, but Velda has found that the impact of a large piece is so much greater than that of a smaller quilt that it makes the extra effort worthwhile. But for this artist, the real challenge is not simply color or size, but coming up with the right design. She spends a lot of time designing and planning. "The sewing part is easy," she says.

Cows in the Meadow is the first quilt Velda made that she designed herself. It is also the first she entered in a contest. The quilt won a special award at that show as well as another prize at a later show. This engaging pastoral scene is cleverly organized so that the fence keeping in the cows is also the quilt's border motif. She used lush velveteen fabric for the cows to give a sense of their glossy hides and created their spots by dropping bleach on the reverse side of the fabric.

Color was the reason for making her award-winning quilt *Hydrangea*, says the artist; "I just couldn't resist the wonderful color of the flowers." Velda hand dyed the background and most of the blues for this quilt to obtain precisely the shades she wanted. Even though the quilter prefers to buy the fabric she needs, she will dye it herself if she cannot find the colors she wants. *Hydrangea* is a lavish marvel of appliqué; the lovely realistic flowers are individually appliquéd, as are the leaves.

Velda's grandmother's flower garden inspired *Iris*, another award-winning quilt. The stately, oversized flowers in this profuse display of irises, ferns, and other plants demand attention and draw the viewer into a sumptuous and luxuriant carnival of colors. The sense of an actual garden is so powerful that you almost expect to smell the flowers. Velda used dyeing and bleaching to achieve just the right hues for the leaves and flowers. She kept the quilting simple so that it does not detract from the major design.

Velda devotes almost all of her spare time to quilting. She teaches and lectures but would rather quilt than teach any day. Her quilts take from three months to a year to complete, depending on the size of the quilt and the complexity of the design and quilting pattern.

Cows in the Meadow; *72 by 84 inches; cotton and velveteen; appliquéd and hand quilted.*

Summer Fragrance; *73 by 86 inches; all-cotton; machine and hand pieced, appliquéd, and hand quilted.*

RUTH M. NORTON

Ruth M. Norton has made quilts for members of her own large family and supplied many brides and new babies with quilted gifts. She has also participated in several major quilt projects. When she heard about the Peace Ribbon, composed of pillowcase-size blocks made by people from all parts of the United States, that was to be tied around the Pentagon in Arlington, Virginia, Ruth volunteered to make a block for Church Women United of Rochester. It represented all the things that we cannot live without: clean air, clean water, plant and animal life, and children. She also made the City Hall block for Rochester's sesquicentennial quilt, and the Town Hall block for a quilt commemorating the town of Irondequoit, where she lives. Ruth's quilts have been winning awards for more than ten years, and they have been shown throughout the country.

Castlewall Medallion, one of Ruth's original designs, was inspired by a book she had read on medallion quilts. She had also been asked to talk to her quilt group about medallion quilts and thought her talk would be a lot more interesting if she had made a medallion quilt and knew just what she was talking about. ''I still have a lot to learn about medallion quilts,'' she says, even though this project resulted in a dazzling and dynamic piece that well represents the genre from her design through her choice of fabric and stitching pattern. The main challenge, she found, was to make new sections fit perfectly; this required a lot of measuring, squeezing, and stretching.

North Country, a design taken from a pattern by Mary Ann Smith and published in a quilting magazine, depicts the starkness and beauty of winter through its careful design and Ruth's choice of fabrics. Using deep greens and soft orchids, grays, tans, blues, and whites, this quilt presents the essence of winter through pine trees that splash color against snow-covered mountains, the Northern Lights that fill winter's long nights with vibrant colors, and the gray days that are brightened by gently falling snow. The quilting, a combination of straight lines, soft curves, circles, and various angles, recalls the wind that whistles and whispers through the winter months.

Summer Fragrance combines flowers and patches in a bouquet of pretty colors and delicate, blossomlike quilting. The pattern, a traditional one published in a quilting magazine, appealed to Ruth because it suggests a happy summer day when flowers are in bloom. She also felt that a scrap quilt offered her a special challenge and decided to use only fabrics that she had in her collection. Ruth chose her prettiest scraps, then sat down to create a balanced assortment of colors without repeating a block. This was not an easy task given the number of blocks required for the quilt. Each block uses both patchwork and appliqué, and the same fabrics are used within the block for each technique.

North Country; *45 by 45 inches; all-cotton; hand pieced and hand quilted.*

Castlewall Medallion; *81 by 94 inches; all-cotton; machine and hand pieced, and hand quilted.*

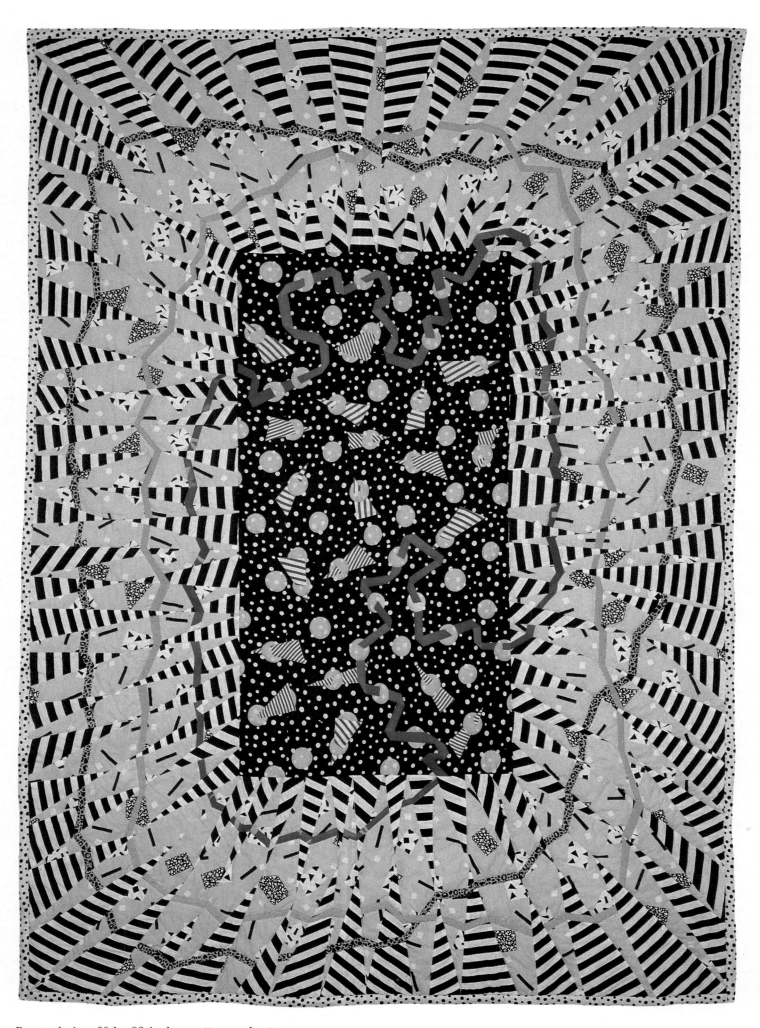

Pyrotechnics; *60 by 82 inches; cotton and cotton blends; machine pieced, machine inlay, and hand and machine quilting.*

ELLEN OPPENHEIMER

Ellen Oppenheimer, who has studied ceramics and glass art, is a self-taught quilter. She learned almost everything she knows about quilts through trial and error. Soon after receiving her undergraduate degree, she made her first quilt from a collection of old ties that her father was throwing away. For that quilt Ellen used traditional blocks, but she quickly found her own original sense of design and now creates large abstract quilts that sparkle with zest and energy. Ellen usually does not start a quilt with a complete design already figured out. She begins with a general idea of what she wants and revises the details as the work progresses. "I am often very anxious toward the end of a quilt," she says. "I am very committed at that point, but I do not know how it will look when it is finally completed." In putting her quilts together, Ellen uses a technique that is similar to reverse appliqué but is done on a sewing machine. "I call this technique machine inlaying," she says. Ellen uses many fabrics just the way they come from the store, but she overdyes others if a quilt requires a specific shade or tone to complement other colors in it.

Ellen had trouble getting started on *Pyrotechnics*; she had just had a show and it was difficult to get another project moving. But the fabric got her going, and she chose to work from the outside in. This presented a challenge, particularly in making the lines meet accurately. The quilt vibrates with vitality that is enhanced by the burst of irregular yellow shapes exploding from the center. The colorful meandering lines running around and through the pattern represent the paths that people follow through their lives.

New Year's Eve Party got started when the artist decided to start the New Year in her studio rather than at a party. For Ellen the quilt became a party with crazy and wonderful fabrics. The curved seams were the special challenge in this quilt as was finding a border color that could hold its own against all the other powerful colors. *Black and White Quilt* started with pencil and ink drawings that Ellen reproduced in fabric. *Bed Quilt* carries the black-and-white motif a step further by adding red. The result is a delightful design, a playful manipulation of perspective that creates a sense of architecture.

Broken Arm Quilt uses a pieced block format and technique rather than machine inlaying. It is playful and exuberant, a story of life's interwoven and overlapping pathways. While she was making this quilt, Ellen fell and broke her arm; she did most of the piecing with her arm in a cast.

Two fabrics, a bright yellow print and a black-and-green mazelike material, inspired the design for *October 17*. The quilt is a tangle of moving and shaking planes. The artist says, "There is no solid frame of reference; it is the confusion of a world where there are no absolute truths." The design, she goes on to say, "is similar to an enormous force picking up the ground and giving it a good shake."

Broken Arm Quilt; *72 by 72 inches; cotton and cotton blends; machine pieced, machine inlay, and hand and machine quilting.*

New Year's Eve Party; *76 by 84 inches; cotton and cotton blends; machine pieced, machine inlay, and hand and machine quilting.*

ELLEN OPPENHEIMER

Bed Quilt; *60 by 79 inches; cotton and cotton
blends; machine pieced, machine inlay, and hand
and machine quilting.*

October 17; *64 by 73 inches; cotton and cotton blends; machine pieced, machine inlay, and hand and machine quilting.*

Black and White Quilt; *84 by 84 inches; cotton and cotton blends; machine pieced, machine inlay, and hand and machine quilting.*

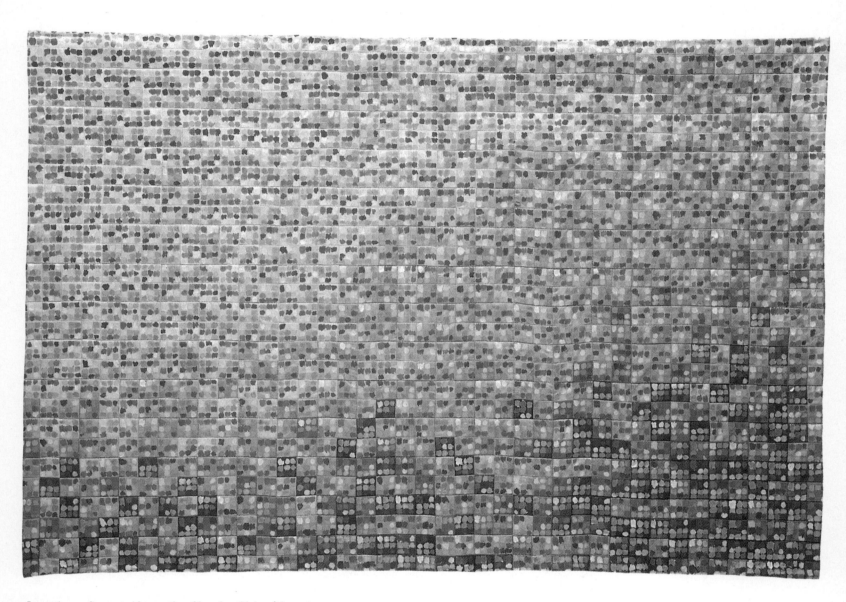

Locations: Sunset Above the Clouds; *61 by 42
inches; cotton and cotton blends; machine pieced
and machine quilted.*

CHERRY PARTEE

Cherry Partee made her first quilt as a wedding present for a close friend. She did not know much about quilting, but she worked in a library and had a steady stream of new books crossing her desk. At the same time she was deciding to make a quilt, *The Mountain Artisans Quilting Book* by Alfred Allan Lewis arrived in the library. "I followed the directions in the book and made the wedding present, and then I just never seemed to stop quilting after that," the artist says.

Recently Cherry has been working on a series of quilts she calls Locations. Each quilt in the series was inspired by a specific place the artist has visited and the memory of the landscape that she carried away with her. The design of each of her Locations quilts is highly abstract and executed in a style reminiscent of a pointillist painting. A myriad of tiny pieces and colors come together to evoke memories for the artist of a specific time and place, and also to pass on to the viewer a sense of participating in the experience. Cherry machine pieced and quilted the quilts in this series, and it took her about 130 hours to make each one, excluding the time she spent on the design. To make these quilts, Cherry used fabrics that she had on hand, finding inspiration for the design in the available colors.

The blazing blues and yellows of *Locations: On the Beach at Noon* shimmer with the heat and radiant energy of sand on a day when the sun is hot, bright, and directly overhead. The touches of white and orange add to the dazzling effect, and there is a sense of water lapping slowly at shore as the tide moves on its inexorable way. Cherry says that the quilt captures the feeling she had when she was at the beach, and while she was making it, she felt the same excitement and happiness she feels when she is at the beach.

Locations: In the Meadow with Red Alder reminds the artist of "the most quiet and peaceful place I have ever been." Although the design was difficult, she found that making the quilt brought her only pleasure. As the soft greens, oranges, and yellows fade into each other, they easily produce the sense of a peaceful field, with just a hint of shadowy saplings near its edges, during the late afternoon of an early summer day.

The stunning quilt *Locations: Sunset Above the Clouds* recalls an airplane trip. Through gradations of vibrant pinks, lavenders, and golds, Cherry captures the shimmering moment of sunset when the plane began its descent and was enveloped by a layer of clouds that glimmered with the reflected light of the beauty and color above. In creating the quilt, the artist recaptured the feeling of excitement that she felt as the plane entered the blush-tinged clouds.

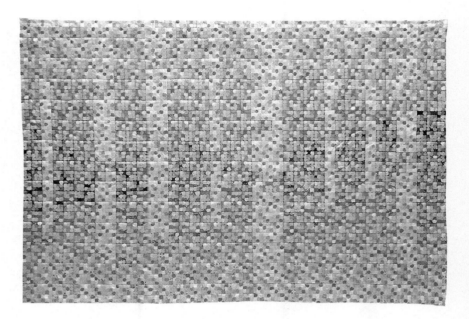

Locations: In the Meadow with Red Alder; *61 by 42 inches; cotton and cotton blends; machine pieced and machine quilted.*

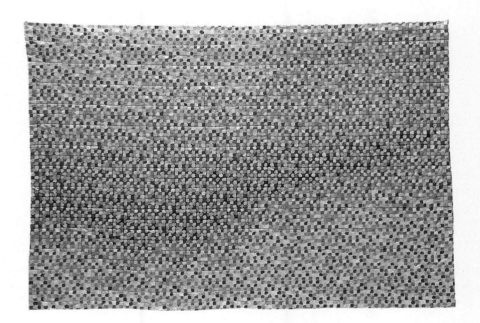

Locations: On the Beach at Noon; *61 by 42 inches; cotton and cotton blends; machine pieced and machine quilted.*

Galactic Gardenia; *72 inches in diameter; cotton, cotton blends, and lamé; machine pieced, reverse appliquéd, and hand quilted. Collection of Kimberly Long Masopust.*

KATIE PASQUINI

Katie Pasquini, who creates richly hued quilts that project three-dimensional illusion and spatial relationships, has always been fascinated by three-dimensional art. Her designs explode with energy and color, and shimmer with an arresting contrast of light and dark. This highly imaginative artist started quilting while she was taking care of her mother. Katie swiftly went from novice to professional quilter as she discovered the delights of this new world of composition and design, and became interested in the various properties of fabrics. Katie transferred her skill and training in painting and drawing to quilt design, rapidly moving from traditional patterns to spectacularly modern designs as she gained greater knowledge of perspective and three-dimensional layouts.

The Juggler is a fascinating study of perspective and seemingly limitless space. It is the last in a series of quilts with spheres and makes use of a strong directional emphasis that draws the viewer's eye from the darker lower-left side of the quilt up through the red diagonal shelf to the floating balls and then down again to the right to follow the bright gold wall out of and back into the quilt. The sense of movement is powerful, but the overall impression of the quilt is peaceful and quiet. The deep shadows and highlighted surfaces imply the existence of a light source outside the quilt that adds significantly to the impression of depth and dimension.

Galactic Gardenia seems to have a light source directly in front of the quilt; the central silver cube shimmers in brightness and the other forms appear to retreat into darkness. The background sphere enhances that impression as its bright golds and oranges gradually change to deeper tones. This quilt has a strong sense of mystery and is reminiscent of the paintings of Victor Vasserely. *Galactic Gardenia*, along with *Atomic Azalea*, is part of Katie's Extraterrestrial Floral series that the artist says is "my idea of what flowers would look like in space." The blossom-shaped black backgrounds of these quilts provide ideal foils for the brilliant colors of the foregrounds.

Atomic Azalea is an irregular sunburst of glorious gradations of color, ranging from light to dark. It is an intense work, and the viewer's eye is continually drawn from its center out to the edge and then back in again along the petals. The quilting follows the planes of some petals and crosses over others, enhancing the impression of depth and dimension in the piece.

Katie spends a part of every day on her work, preparing lectures and class material as well as designing and making new quilts. Because of a heavy teaching schedule that has taken her throughout the United States and to Canada, Belgium, Japan, Australia, New Zealand, and England, she often does not have as much time as she would like for cutting and sewing.

The Juggler; *80 by 72 inches; cotton, cotton blends, silk, and lamé; machine pieced and hand quilted.*

Atomic Azalea; *72 inches in diameter; cotton, cotton blends, and lamé; machine pieced and hand quilted. Collection of Kimberly Long Masopust.*

Soundings; *57 by 70 inches; cotton, cotton blends, silk, and metallics; machine pieced, hand appliquéd, and machine quilted.*

LINDA S. PERRY

Can a high school math teacher find happiness making quilts? Linda S. Perry believes one can and she does. While she was on leave from teaching to be home with her infant son, Linda went to a show of contemporary quilts and was overwhelmed, finding the colors and the designs spectacular and appealing. She recognized the mathematical complexity underpinning many of the designs, and she knew she had found her medium.

Along the way to becoming a math teacher, Linda had taken many art courses. She had also worked briefly as an illustrator, so Linda was no stranger to many of the design concepts that are expressed through contemporary quilts. Another reason she knew that quilting was for her was that ever since she could remember Linda had loved fabric: "Just going into a fabric store makes my heart beat faster," she says.

The quiltmaker loves Art Deco and Japanese design, and the influence of these styles is evident in much of her work. Her quilt *Leda* elegantly combines elements that recall the sharp angles and dramatic curves of the 1920s and the subtle gradations in texture and color that reflect the sensibilities found in Japanese country textiles. The quilt also reflects Linda's fascination with Greek mythology. When she chose to depict the story of Leda, she knew she wanted to show the mystical and transcendent aspect of the myth but recognized that she could easily become trapped in a literal or figurative depiction of the tale. She decided to represent Leda with a circle of sensuously patterned fabrics and to overlay green face shapes with oak leaves, the symbol of Leda's lover, Zeus. Leda's twin sons, Castor and Pollux, are represented by the constellation Gemini, and the bright red triangle floating in space stands for the bloodshed and anguish caused by the incomparable Helen of Troy, another offspring of Leda and the god.

Benthic Fans and *Soundings* are two very distinct designs inspired by the artist's love for the ocean. "I am fascinated," she says, "by the spectacular colors and forms of the organisms found in the deep." Bright and unusual colors and languorous curved shapes, based on two-sided fans, are combined in these quilts to give a sense of the continual ebb and flow of ocean currents, as well as the immense and mysterious space that the little-known creatures of the deep inhabit. In making these quilts, Linda found herself frequently reminded of Christopher Newbert's book *Within a Rainbowed Sea*. To achieve the effect she wanted in these quilts, the artist had to hand print or hand dye fabric. She hunted far and wide to find precisely the right fabric for the borders of *Benthic Fans* and ended up hand printing the black and silver that she wanted. For the background of *Soundings*, she found that only hand dyeing could give her the subtle gradations that implied the transitions between ocean depths.

Benthic Fans; *52 by 66½ inches; cotton, cotton blends, silk, and metallics; machine pieced, hand appliquéd, and machine quilted.*

Leda; *38 by 47½ inches; cotton, silk, wool, and metallic thread; machine pieced, hand appliquéd, and machine quilted.*

Kaleidoscope; *83 by 103 inches; cotton and cotton blends; machine pieced and machine quilted.*

BARBARA RICKEY

When members of Barbara Rickey's church decided to make a quilt for a raffle, she signed up for the committee even though she knew nothing about quilting. Barbara was an experienced seamstress, and by the time the church project was finished, she had read every book on quilting that she could find in the library, done a lot of experimenting, and come to the conclusion that making quilts was how she wanted to spend the rest of her life. Along with many quilts and wall hangings, Barbara has made six church banners that represent different seasons of the Christian year.

Lancaster County Rose was the first quilt Barbara made all by herself. Barbara calls it a "quilt-as-you-go" project for which she quilted the individual blocks as she made them, then machine pieced them together with pieced sashing. She also quilted the borders individually and added them last. In this quilt the appliquéd blocks are composed of ten different combinations of pink fabrics; each is repeated once, given green print leaves, and appliquéd by machine to a muslin ground. While she was doing the machine appliqué, the quiltmaker placed a piece of heavy butcher paper under each square; this prevented the sewing machine from drawing up the fabric, but it was difficult to remove the paper after the appliqué was completed. "The whole family was involved in tearing it away," Barbara recalls. "We even tried wetting the paper to make it tear more easily."

Even though it has a contemporary look, Barbara's quilt *Churn Dash* is a variation on a traditional pattern. Setting it with muslin strips was the artist's own idea. The quilting design she used is also original; Barbara developed it to enhance the pieced design. The artist used only medium to dark values of certain color families—pinks through purple reds and lavender blues. After piecing all the blocks, she laid them out and moved them around to achieve the most pleasing arrangement of colors. At the time Barbara made this quilt, she was teaching scrap quilt classes, and she began the quilt to demonstrate color organization. All the materials for the quilt top came from her extensive fabric inventory.

Kaleidoscope is another outgrowth of the artist's scrap-quilt teaching. The fabrics came from her collection that she sorted into lights and darks, choosing to use few medium values. She then positioned the fabrics within the traditional block in such a way that a secondary pattern of interlocking circles and large four-pointed stars was created when the blocks were put together. The top was machine quilted with transparent nylon filament thread. While Barbara found that quilting this piece was not difficult, at times it was exasperating because there was such a large body of work to handle. She says that she loves what she does so much that she almost never gets discouraged with any phase of quiltmaking, but some parts just take longer than others or are more of a challenge.

Churn Dash; *96 by 105 inches; cotton and cotton blends; machine pieced and hand quilted.*

Lancaster County Rose; *80 by 94 inches; cotton and cotton blends; machine pieced, appliquéd, and hand quilted.*

City Lights; *45 by 56 inches; all-cotton; machine pieced and hand quilted.*

JOAN M. RIGAL

The first quilt that Joan M. Rigal ever made was exhibited in the Toledo Art Museum, where she took her first quiltmaking class. Her teacher encouraged the students to develop their own designs, and Joan created a quilt composed entirely of parallelograms. After six months' work on the full-size quilt, she had the honor of seeing it exhibited. Joan still laughs when she remembers a guard asking her please not to touch the quilt as it hung in the museum.

"I like to take traditional designs and do something different with them," says Joan, and she has followed up her first quilt with many others, including one that depicts a little sailboat that looks like one her children used to play with. Today her quilts tend to be more abstract, but Joan has always been fascinated by Amish design and color combinations, and many of her pieces seem to have been inspired by Amish quilts.

City Lights was the first quilt that Joan submitted to a juried show (it won second place). She used the Ohio Star pattern as the starting point and then "pushed it all together." Joan began her design with the color combination in the middle block and says that she had no idea she would end up using all the other colors. The black border and the twin diamonds of yellow green at the corners of the outer blocks create a sparkling contrast with the graded tones of the rest of the quilt. Because the colors are so strong, Joan kept the quilting simple, so that it gives dimension and depth, enhancing and not detracting from the colors.

Joan's quilt *Rosanne's Poppies* is a softly glowing medley of subtle solid colors. This small wall quilt has a nine-patch pieced center. The quilt is a reminder of a poppy plant Joan received from her sister-in-law many years ago. She planted this wonderful gift near her kitchen door and watched the plant bloom year after year. "I loved it, so it was easy to remember just how the flowers should look when I was working on the quilt in the winter," Joan says. She cut the poppies from the bias of the material, then added embroidery and beading. The ground of the quilt was inspired by Amish designs, and the poppies were an afterthought. "As I was quilting, I thought how much the colors reminded me of Oriental poppies, so I ripped out the quilting, added the poppies, and started the quilting again." This time, Joan used a stitching pattern that carried through the theme. The decision to rip out the quilting and add the flowers was not made lightly; it was discouraging, time-consuming, and hard to do. But the result was well worth the effort.

Her quilt *Amish* is based on the traditional Sunshine and Shadow pattern. Joan used all-cotton fabric for this wall quilt to produce a jewellike impact. The combination of deep, pure colors and the intricate fine quilting that radiates from the center gives the effect of faceted stones.

Rosanne's Poppies; *30 by 34 inches; all-cotton and beads; machine pieced, embroidered, and hand quilted.*

Amish; *39¾ by 46¾ inches; all-cotton; machine pieced and hand quilted.*

145

Orange Blossom; *85 by 104 inches; all-cotton;
machine pieced, appliquéd, and hand quilted.*

KATHRYN ROUSE

Kathryn Rouse is a skillful quilter who has so many interests in addition to quilting that a quilt can take her as long as two years to complete. Kathryn has a degree in early childhood education and taught in Montessori schools for 11 years. Today she teaches English as a second language and does volunteer work at a health care agency, so she is not always able to devote as much time as she might like to quilting.

Kathryn enjoys both appliqué and patchwork, but her particular talent is fine hand quilting. Her quilt *Orange Blossom*, with its gently curved lines and minimal design, is an especially elegant example of her exquisite quilting. Kathryn found this design in a 1930s pattern book and adapted the traditional quilting pattern to better fit the design. Marking the top for quilting was the most difficult part of making the quilt. Her tiny and precise stitches, reminiscent of fancywork of a bygone era, create graceful, flowing feather patterns that provide a gentle counterpoint to the simple orange-blossom appliqué. The off-white ground is the perfect foil for the densely stitched patterns, allowing the quilt to achieve an overall sense of depth and dimension. The feather motif also highlights and complements the softly rounded corners of the quilt. Kathryn carried out the orange-blossom design with delicately patterned calicos, and this choice of fabric gives additional texture to a design often executed entirely in solids. This extraordinary quilt, which was the first of her quilts that Kathryn felt was technically good enough to enter in a show, won second place at the 1988 Wisconsin State Fair and best of show at the 1988 Wandering Foot Quilters Show.

Tumbling Blocks is a more robust example of this quilter's work. The piece is based on a traditional patchwork pattern, but Kathryn has used a subtle palette offset with black to create a striking new variation of the theme. She prefers all-cotton fabrics, but in this quilt Kathryn decided to use cotton blends because their highly polished surfaces suggest the lustrous silk, velvet, and satin Crazy Quilts made around the turn of the century. She backed the quilt with pure cotton because "that feels better against your skin," she says. The many small pieces that make up the quilt were hand stitched together. Unlike the elaborate quilting she used in *Orange Blossom*, this quilt is stitched with a simple grid pattern that complements the bold design in an understated manner.

Unlike some quilters, Kathryn buys quilt fabrics specifically for a design. When she used to make her own clothes, she would buy fabric on impulse, thinking that someday she might find a use for it, but she rarely did. Now she is more cautious, remembering how easy it is to end up with a mountain of fabrics that are never right for the project at hand.

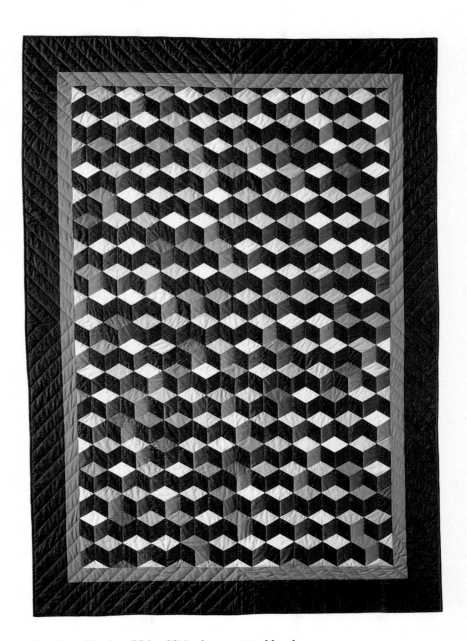

Tumbling Blocks; *55 by 77 inches; cotton blends; hand pieced and hand quilted.*

Orange Blossom *(detail).*

Star of Bluegrass; *85 by 96 inches; cotton blends;*
hand pieced and hand quilted.

148

ROSE SANDERS

Rose Sanders became interested in quilts after she bought an old rope bed and decided that she wanted an authentic bed cover for it—preferably a quilt. She could not find the quilt she wanted at flea markets or auctions, and when she finally saw the perfect quilt at a quilt show, it turned out not to be for sale. Since she did not know any quilters, Rose decided to make the quilt she wanted. She bought the pattern and went to work. Her lovely *Star of Bluegrass* quilt took Rose more than a year to make, but she feels that the result was well worth the effort, especially since it has won three awards.

When Rose started quilting, she had no idea of what she was getting into, since the only other needlework she had made was crewel and embroidery. But the difficult and sometimes frustrating and intimidating process of creating the quilt gave her a sense of accomplishment, and she has gone on to make seven quilts. "I truly believe in quality, not quantity," Rose says, and she always devotes whatever length of time is necessary to ensure that her quilts receive the meticulous care they deserve.

Rose uses traditional patterns or her own variations because she wants to be sure that the hallmarks of the tradition are preserved for the future. She is especially fond of the heavy and intricate quilting that sets antique quilts apart from some of the quilts that have been made recently. When she designs or chooses a quilt pattern, she gravitates toward the one that offers the most opportunity for quilting and will best feature the stitching design.

"Most people start with quilt blocks, but not me," she says. Her first quilt, *Star of Bluegrass*, was a complex project for a novice. "After the first two rows were together, I knew something was wrong with the design. Finally, I realized that the light blue and dark blue stars in the center were not all turned the same way. I had to remove a lot of stitches to fix this problem." Her next quilt, *Crown of Cerise*, has a beguiling, old-fashioned appearance, enhanced by swags that border the main design and charming print "birds" that seem to fly from fruit to fruit. The piece has a simple, symmetrical look in which the colors and motif join to produce a strong folk art effect. Rose also wanted to keep the colors subdued to augment the antique look of the quilt. The quilting carries out the main motif and offers its own glorious contribution to the overall effect. The artist admits that the extensive appliqué required by the design was difficult; she experimented with the cherries for a long time before adding them to the quilt.

Because Rose is a mother, adores horseback riding and show jumping, and attends college, she does not always have a quilt in the works. But when she is quilting, she gets up at five o'clock and works on her quilt until ten. "And sometimes at night as well, if I'm not too pooped," she says.

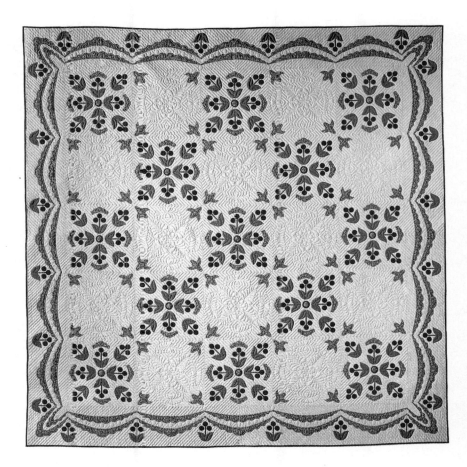

Crown of Cerise; *94 by 94 inches; all-cotton; appliquéd and hand quilted.*

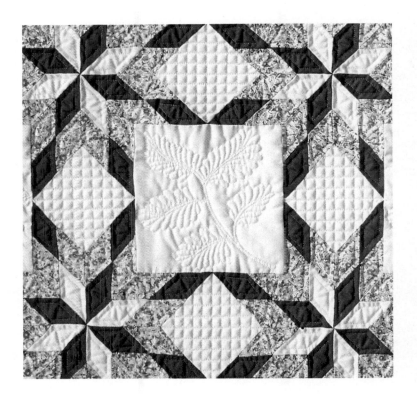

Star of Bluegrass *(detail).*

Quasar; 49 by 60 inches; cotton and cotton blends;
machine pieced, appliquéd, and hand quilted.

STEPHANIE SANTMYERS

Stephanie Santmyers has developed her own unique style of quiltmaking that she calls the Master Template method. She develops a set of between 11 and 15 templates and then uses only those templates to create a design for the quilt blocks she is making. The template determines the size of each area, but the artist pieces each area in the way she chooses, as long as the piecing fits the template. "By freeing myself from many small, complex templates," she says, "I can introduce small variations or change my ideas in progress."

Stephanie's dazzling abstract designs that are often created from four large mirror-image blocks seem to explode from the boundaries of her quilts in a profusion of pattern and color. This mostly self-taught artist made her first quilt, an original design that looks traditional, while her husband was on an extended overseas trip in 1982. A few years later after taking a five-day workshop with the well-known quilter Nancy Crow, Stephanie realized that quilts did not have to have traditional designs. She has now produced 11 traditional quilts of her own design and 13 art quilts in the extraordinary designs that have become her hallmark.

Stephanie used the same template for both *Sanduleak 202 -69° 1987A* and *Quasar*. Science fiction and thermophotography, in which astronomers use infrared color photography to study celestial events, suggested the designs for these quilts. "Astral space is my metaphor for those things unexpected but real in the imagination, for the colors and patterns that the mind knows but the eye has not seen," Stephanie says. She wanted her quilts to reflect a realm of comets, novas, and voyaging alien space ships— "places of mystery and freedom"—as well as the spectrum of glorious colors seen with thermophotography. *Sanduleak* represents the exploding star or nova by that name seen by astronomers in 1987. In designing the quilt, the artist used more solid colors than usual. *Quasar* is an expression of the movement and power of light, and Stephanie quilted with silver thread in some places to augment this impression. *Africa* is also a template quilt, but it reflects African art rather than outer space. In this quilt the artist combined cottons with curtain and upholstery fabrics to provide interest and texture, and her choice of prints enhances the perception of tribal arts.

Drawing the design and then translating it into fabric and color are the hardest part of quiltmaking for Stephanie. "I spend most of my creative time pinning the work on a wall, composing the colors and patterned cloth. My working drawing is a value study of gray, black, and white—no color." Her designs, she says, are a little like working on a jigsaw puzzle. "Finding the corners and the edges is easy in a puzzle but working in the center is difficult. The quilt is just the opposite—the center is usually easy, but as pieces of the design are added, keying in new parts becomes more and more difficult."

Sanduleak 202 -69° 1987A; *56 by 59 inches; cotton and cotton blends; machine pieced and hand quilted.*

Africa; *58 by 67 inches; cotton and cotton blends; machine pieced, appliquéd, and hand quilted.*

Garden Spiral; *50 by 50 inches; cotton and lamé;*
machine pieced, appliquéd, and machine quilted.

JANE A. SASSAMAN

Jane A. Sassaman has worked as a sign maker, window dresser, illustrator, and designer of decorative accessories. She has also painted, done embroidery, and made soft sculpture. But now she is a quilter and finds that it gives her the elements she most liked in other media. "I learned by making mistakes," says this self-taught quilter, "but I have a natural ability for precision."

Jane's vibrant and exciting quilts explore subtle metaphysical images and concepts, and have drawn substantial attention at juried and invitational shows. Some of her quilts are on extended national and international tours; others hang in corporate and private collections around the country. *Garden Spiral*, one of her quilts that is currently on tour, is a dramatically crafted piece. Its strong diagonals convey movement and growth, reminiscent of plants coming to life in the spring, while the bright and sparkling colors represent that new life against the black "earth" ground of the quilt. Jane spent a long time designing this quilt, but she says, "The ideas that came through during the design process are still influencing my current work.

Jane's quilt *Dark Study* is part of a series that celebrates a mystical universe. She used gold hand-painted accents partly because gold has significance in many cultural and religious ceremonies and partly because of its rich and heavenly attributes. Jane made this quilt while she was a guest resident at the Junior Museum of the Art Institute of Chicago. It is a small work compared with many of her pieces because it was made for a specific space in the museum. "The challenge," she says, "was to make a big statement in a small quilt.

Currently, this artist is exploring the concept of radiation in her work. The connotations of *radiation* are both negative (radioactive nuclear waste) and positive (light from the sun), but Jane is interested in the positive. "Consider the radiation of the sun or the soul or the spirit," she says. "Radiation can be divine or sublime, *inspirational* as well as *expirational.*" *Divine Radiation*, a provocative quilt in this series, projects energy and strength; it reaches for a positive expression of the concept and represents the relationship between heaven and earth that is grasped in moments of enlightenment which make us one with the universe. Like all her quilts, this one is not made up of blocks. Each section is an irregular shape, and Jane had to put them together in a particular order to get them to fit in their assigned positions.

"When my children were babies," Jane recalls, "it took forever to finish a quilt—I was working free lance, too. Once it took me three years to hand quilt one large quilt." Now, she has made almost thirty quilts, her children are older and more self-reliant, and the artist is a full-time quilter who devotes at least eight hours a day to quilting. She says that she is not happy unless she is working.

Dark Study; *36 by 36 inches; all-cotton; machine pieced, appliquéd, and machine quilted.*

Divine Radiation; *69 by 63 inches; cotton and cotton blends; machine pieced, appliquéd, and machine quilted.*

ROBIN SCHWALB

Projectionist Please Focus; *43 by 59 inches;*
all-cotton photo-silkscreened and stenciled fabric;
machine and hand pieced, appliquéd, and hand
quilted.

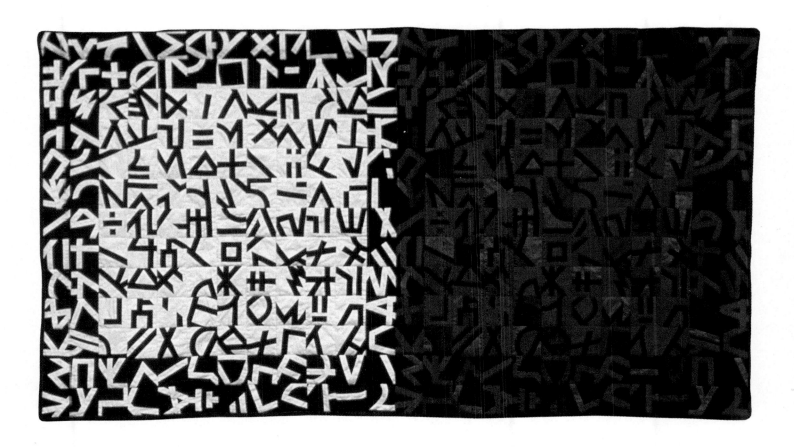

Let X = X; *72 by 39 inches; cotton and cotton
blends; machine pieced and hand quilted.*

PCB Bop; *55 by 41 inches; all-cotton and metal
studs; machine and hand pieced, appliquéd, and
hand quilted.*

The Calendar Fetish: An Altar to Time; *60 by 84
by 3 inches; cotton, cotton blends, silk, satin,
lamé, velvet, buttons, and other embellishments;
hand pieced, appliquéd, and hand quilted.
Collection of Ardis and Robert James.*

SUSAN SHIE

Susan Shie's vibrant and exciting quilts are an unrestrained visual feast. Through multifaceted and unusual abstract collages, she explores personal relationships, symbolism, spirituality, and healing. Sewing has always been a part of Susan's life. Her mother sewed regularly, and at the age of three or four, Susan began to "fool around" with a needle and thread. She made doll clothes and her own clothes, and went to Ladies Aid quilt days with her mother. While she was growing up, Susan was also interested in drawing, painting, and crafts. In college she began to merge sewing and painting in her studio art. If Susan wants to sew with the accuracy of a perfectionist like her mother, she can, but Susan has developed a looser, less structured technique that creates highly textured quilts. She says that as a painter she sees big stitches as more comparable to brush strokes.

The Calendar Fetish: An Altar to Time is a striking and playful collage of movable pieces. The artist says that this piece is "the first and only perpetual calendar quilt." Months, days, holidays, and lunar phases are all included, and the pieces can be moved around and refastened with buttons to keep the calendar accurate from month to month. This colorful melange of materials and objects is a lighthearted comment on the current popularity of calendars on any and every theme. Even though she had trouble getting all the elements of the calendar to fit into the space, Susan refused to become discouraged: "I figured that if it didn't work, I could always save the parts and use them later."

Back to Eden: A Green Quilt is another stimulating and exciting collage. It is the first quilt Susan made in collaboration with her husband. This unique combination of unexpected techniques includes tooled and painted leather animals that are sewn to quilted hidden pockets, hanks of embroidery thread that emphasize the large stitches, and crystals. The largest crystal is on the central figure of copper fabric, who represents the Great Mother from a Native American creation myth. The turtle figure above her is stuffed and appliquéd. The bottom panel recalls Edward Hicks's Peaceable Kingdom paintings.

River in the Sky has Halley's Comet as its basic theme, but the artist, who was working on the quilt at the time of the Challenger disaster, felt that she could not complete it without paying tribute to the space shuttle's crew. She included them on the left side of the background panel, giving their figures wings. "Comet people" and "high-speed angels" also fly across the quilt, and wildly striped iridescent fabric is a reminder that this was the Year of the Tiger in Chinese astrology. Long, torn strips of fabric serving as huge border "stitches" overlay the entire work, giving it a sense of continual action and movement.

Back to Eden: A Green Quilt; *80 by 78 by 3 inches; cotton, leather, fabrics of unknown origin, and crystal; hand pieced, appliquéd, and hand quilted. Made in collaboration with James Acord. Collection of Nancy and Darryl Siebert.*

River in the Sky; *144 by 84 by 3 inches; cotton, cotton blends, silk, mylar, fabrics of unknown origin, clothespins, and other embellishments; hand pieced, appliquéd, and hand quilted.*

Becky's Paper Doll; *45 by 54 inches; cotton, cotton blends, beads, and embroidery floss; hand pieced, reverse appliquéd, and hand quilted.*

REBEKKA SIEGEL

Rebekka Siegel's complex and colorful quilts always tell a story. More than anything, she says, her quilts represent the inspiration that she receives from the people with whom she shares her life. Rebekka mostly uses appliqué and reverse appliqué to make quilts, but she does not ignore traditional piecework techniques. She has used such techniques as Seminole patchwork, batik, and direct dye to create the images and colors that she wants in her pieces. Her neat and tiny stitching often forms straight lines and simple patterns that complement rather than overshadow her central theme, but occasionally she uses stitching to provide an additional element to the design, such as waves in a pond or clouds in the sky.

The artist's creative handling of a central theme is evident in *Snakes in the Garden of Eden*. This quilt is replete with biblical symbolism, but Rebekka's young son also supplied inspiration for its creation through his fascination with snakes, which Rebekka eventually came to share. As she began to recognize their beauty, Rebekka found herself drawn to the idea of a quilt that would highlight the snake's sinuous form and decided that the Garden of Eden provided an appropriate theme. The quilt combines old and new by bringing together the traditional Garden of Eden block, pieced in lush tones of garden greens, and the multiple and lively appliquéd snakes, focusing their attention on a large and obviously tempting apple. Rebekka is not constrained by the edges of her central field and lets her snakes flow over the borders and even beyond; some of them seem to ignore the confines of the quilt itself. The fabric used for each snake is different, and Rebekka collected her material from quilters in all parts of the country and Australia through a quilters' chain letter.

Rebekka says that *Becky's Paper Doll* is a very personal quilt, inspired by her childhood love of paper dolls. Both the paper doll at the quilt's center and the figure of the little girl at work with her scissors in one corner of the quilt represent the quilter herself. The doll's outfits are based on clothes that Rebekka wore as a youngster, and each of them is a small quilt in its own right, attached to the larger quilt with a Velcro backing. This quilt allows you actually to play paper dolls and change the doll's clothes. The irregular white patches are meant to be scraps of leftover paper, and Rebekka embellished these areas with symbols of other playthings that were important to her when she was a child. The border on this quilt incorporates scissors as a clever design element that ties together the long rows of little girl cutouts at the corners. Rebekka says that although she never got discouraged during the three months she worked on this quilt, she did get a little bored appliquéing all those little girls around the border.

Snakes in the Garden of Eden; *58 by 74 inches; cotton, cotton blends, buttons, and beads; machine pieced, appliquéd, and hand quilted.*

Becky's Paper Doll *(detail)*.

The Fascinating Ladies of Bygone Baltimore; *79 by 79 inches; cotton and silk; appliquéd and hand quilted. Contributing quilters: Jeanne Benson, June Dixon, Zollalee Amos Gaylor, Eloise Lewis McCartney, Kathy Pease, and Albertine Veenstra; quilting by Hazel B. Reed Ferrell.*

ELLY SIENKIEWICZ

Elly Sienkiewicz has taken a nineteenth century tradition and brought it up to date with the dedicated help of enthusiastic quilters from around the country. This artist has long been fascinated with Baltimore Album quilts; she is the author of a series of books about these quilts and the techniques and patterns that were used to create them. In 1983 her first Baltimore Album book inspired a contest, with the winners becoming the modern-day Ladies of Baltimore, an ongoing and ever-growing group of quilters.

Elly learned how to quilt from her great-aunt. But before she made quilting her career, Elly taught history and English for seven years. After another seven years of teaching quilting and running a mail-order quilt supply shop, she sold her business so that she could pursue her interest in teaching and writing about Baltimore Album quilts. Elly teaches the techniques, from appliqué to calligraphy and fraktur, that a quilter must know to produce blocks similar to those found in historic Baltimore Album quilts.

Elly and the winners of the first Album quilt contest have brought together the past and the present of quiltmaking by creating several appliquéd Album quilts in which the design, execution, beauty, color, and complexity rival those made in the mid-nineteenth century. Like the original Baltimore quilts, these modern versions have such characteristic design elements as intricate florals, hearts, patriotic symbols, trailing vines, pictorial blocks, and writing. Sometimes, the quilters are totally faithful to tradition; at other times, they add contemporary touches, particularly in the picture blocks.

Ten winners of the contest made 15 blocks of *The Good Ladies of Baltimore*, and Elly made the other ten. Even though it was a group-made quilt inspired by the contest, the enthusiasm and generosity of the quiltmakers turned it into something more. Elly coordinated the project and set the blocks into a coherent overall design. She also chose to make the quilt not only an album of fond memories of the quilters who participated but also a family album, with the blocks above and below the center one showing her daughter with her two cats and her husband and herself in front of their home.

The Fascinating Ladies of Bygone Baltimore contains blocks made by five of the contest winners, seven blocks by Elly, and the four-block central medallion by another quilter. Three of the blocks are particularly ornate, containing folded silk flowers, ruched flowers, and other special appliqué techniques. Elly designed and set the quilt; the position of the central medallion and the border are based on an antique quilt. She also designed the border corners, which were not part of the original design, to match the center. This quilt was intended to be a groom's gift for one of her sons, and his silhouette and those of other family members are included on one of the blocks.

The Good Ladies of Baltimore; *91 by 91 inches; cotton, silk, and lamé; appliquéd and hand quilted. Contributing quilters: Jeanne Benson, Agnes Cook, Nonna Crock, June Dixon, Zollalee Amos Gaylor, Jeana Kimball, Eloise Lewis McCartney, Sylvia Pickell, Mary Toda, and Albertine Veenstra; quilting by Virginia Lemasters and Carol Jo White.*

The Fascinating Ladies of Bygone Baltimore *(detail)*.

163

Dance of the Sprites; *58 by 68 inches; all-cotton; machine pieced and machine quilted.*

LOIS TORNQUIST SMITH

Sampler quilts are Lois Tornquist Smith's specialty, but she has made many other kinds of quilts including a pictorial quilt that shows scenes of Washington, D.C. Even though Lois often designs quilts with traditional blocks, the end result is a fabric collage that blends and unites the shades and textures of traditional and contemporary quilting and yields a wholly new and beautiful creation. Lois often textures her fabrics in some way to add even more interest to her quilts.

In *Heritage*, a sampler quilt that was made as a wedding gift for one of her children, Lois has captured the history and memories of three generations in a compelling combination of traditional and original blocks. The quilt sends a message of love and welcome to the newest member of the family, while providing a wealth of family history. A Family Tree block remembers the births and deaths of the last hundred years. Another block shows the bride and groom, their wedding cake, and the Smith family. The Popcorn block recalls a Sunday-evening family ritual (Lois used elastic thread to translate muslin into believable popcorn), and Fourth of July remembers lively celebrations at the Washington Monument. The border recalls Lois's mother, who was skillful at braiding rugs. Some of the blocks are ones traditionally included in a wedding quilt, but they have their own meaning for this family. The Clam Shell block represents happy days at the beach; Spools is for the needle arts. Hunter's Star brings to mind days of hunting enjoyed by Lois's son, and Union is for the marriage.

The soft pastels in *Dance of the Sprites*, which range from graded tones to light and clear colors, required hand dyeing to obtain exactly the right shades. Lois used a Pinwheel block as the basis for her design but placed the blocks so that the pinwheels interlock. For Lois the pinwheels represent souls, or sprites, and the artist envisions them as gaining energy as they spin their way to eternity. This was the artist's first color wash project, and she found that she had to lay out every piece of fabric before sewing them together to insure that the colors would fall in the right places.

In her sampler quilt *Asian Delights*, Lois modifies traditional American blocks to carry out a Japanese theme. The Ocean Waves block, for example, contains a stitched Japanese ocean wave crest in the center, and the classic Nine Patch is transformed into a Japanese Lantern block. A block the artist calls Kimono is a copy of a patchwork coat made for a sixteenth-century general, and two other blocks make use of coasters, given to her daughter by a visitor from Japan, that depict faces from Japanese woodblock prints. Elegant fans adorn the space between the blocks, and Meander stitching adds depth and dimension to the sashing and background. Lois developed this quilt after purchasing a Japanese floral fabric that inspired her to learn more about that country's culture and art.

Heritage; *93 by 93 inches; all-cotton; machine pieced and machine quilted.*

Asian Delights; *83 by 99 inches; all-cotton; machine pieced, appliquéd, and machine quilted.*

Bear's Paw; *85 by 110 inches; all-cotton; hand pieced and hand quilted. Collection of Ginger Neusel.*

SMOKEY MOUNTAIN QUILTERS

S mokey Mountain Quilters, a chapter of the Tennessee Valley Quilters' Association and the National Quilting Association, is an energetic and dynamic group of quilters who are carrying on an important and rewarding part of the American quilting tradition—the quilting bee. Inspired by Allison Arnold, a nationally accredited quilting teacher who lives in the area, the group was started in 1980 by 17 women who wanted the opportunity to share their interests and enthusiasms with other quilters. The group immediately hit a sympathetic chord with quilters in the area, and Smokey Mountain Quilters now has 100 members, who range in age from their early twenties to late sixties and exhibit all levels of expertise.

The group makes one quilt every year for an annual show. It is raffled, and the proceeds are used to defray the show's expenses. If any money is leftover, it is spent to bring quilt experts to teach and talk during the weekly bees. The pattern for the raffle quilt is chosen by the group, so the quilt is a group effort from start to finish. Usually, almost everyone in the chapter, regardless of which bee she goes to, puts in some time on the raffle quilt.

The Bear's Paw is the logo of the Smokey Mountain Quilters, so it was easy for the group to decide to make the raffle quilt *Bear's Paw*. The 22 quilters who made it had no trouble working together. The hard part of this quilt was getting enough blue print fabric to complete the design. The group's favorite fabric was a remnant that was no longer easily available, and it took calls to 15 companies to get enough of the print to make the quilt.

Quintet is a scrap quilt, and the quilters purchased only the fabric for the small tan squares. The original design called for the exclusive use of earth tones with no blues, greens, or lavenders. But not everyone managed to adhere to the guidelines, and the deviations in color add verve and sparkle to the quilt. This quilt was made by 53 quilters, and like all raffle quilts, it symbolizes love, friendship, and unity of spirit.

Usually, the pattern comes first in making a quilt, but fabrics inspired *Banbury Cross*. The quilters found Hoffman fabrics so powerful and dynamic that they decided to use a block that would showcase several of them, and the result is a stunning interplay of color and design. The quilting pattern chosen looks simple but it isn't; each of the 21 quilters recalls a lot of ripping out as they started the quilting process. They finally made separate templates to help them know where they were.

The Smokey Mountain Quilters also make ''cuddle quilts'' for the local Ronald McDonald House. The group keeps a closet full of quilts, and any child in the program can choose a quilt from the closet. The quilters have a commitment to keep the closet full, and to date they have given away more than two hundred quilts.

Banbury Cross; *93 by 94 inches; all-cotton; hand pieced and hand quilted. Collection of Rebecca Harris.*

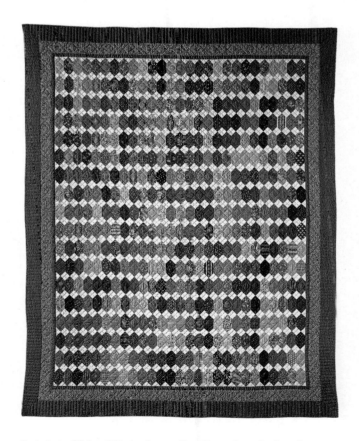

Quintet; *80 by 101 inches; all-cotton; hand pieced and hand quilted. Collection of Ginger Neusel.*

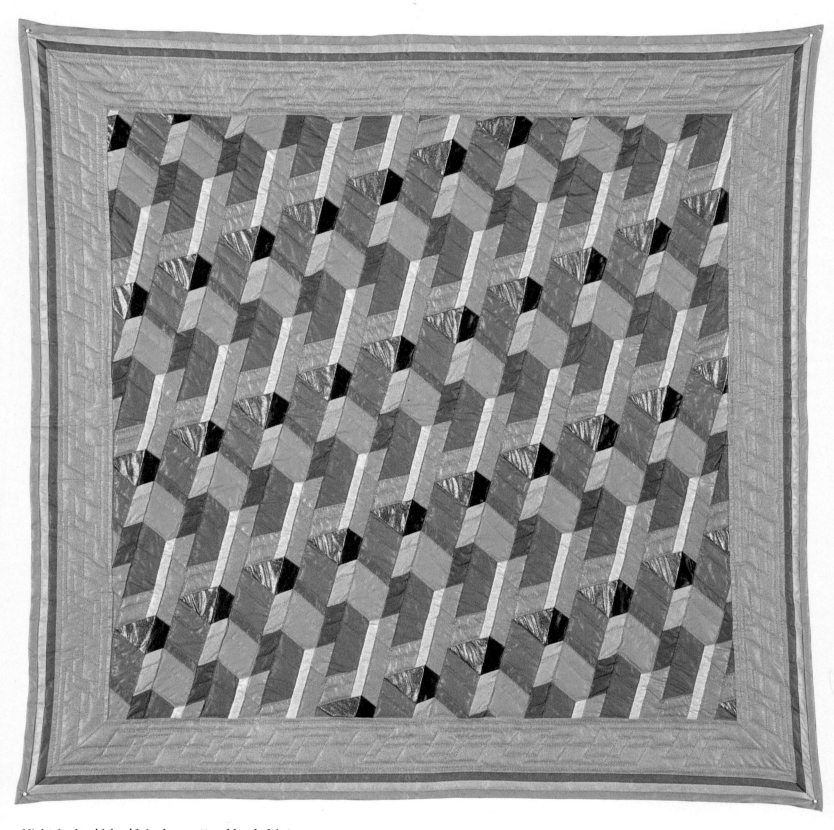

Nightshade; *41 by 41 inches; cotton-blend chintz and tricot lamé; machine pieced and hand quilted.*

REBECCA SPEAKES

Rebecca Speakes uses a T square and an adjustable triangle to create quilts made up of unusual trapezoids, triangles, parallelograms, and hexagons. "I love experiencing the many ways particular shapes fit together," she says, "and I love the challenge of doing the seemingly impossible in making colors and patterns fit together." Scale is also an important factor in this artist's design, since she uses between 13 and 28 pieces for each pattern repeat and the pieces must be large enough to balance the boldness of both color and pattern. This former art and mathematics student took up quiltmaking after designing and crocheting clothes for eight years. She decided that she wanted to move to a medium that had greater design flexibility than the vertical and horizontal planes of crochet. With sewing skills learned from her grandmother, experience as a graphic artist, and a course in quilting backing her up, Rebecca was ready to make dazzling quilts.

Vineyard is an unconventional quilt in the shape of an equilateral triangle. Even though the pattern repeats, there are no traditional blocks; each repeat is like a part of an interlocking puzzle. The triangular format allows the quilt to be viewed from any direction, causing the pattern to produce a variety of different and exciting effects. For this quilt Rebecca used chintz and lamé. "I love the shiny quality of chintz and the hard finish of lamé," she says. "The fabrics work together, softening the colors and blending them." For the artist this quilt is a symbol of the richness of nature that she sees in plants, animals, and geologic formations.

Rebecca's quilt *Timberline* is also constructed on an interlocking grid. There are no regular blocks, so the patterns form irregular shapes. This quilt is contained within traditional rectangular borders and gives an impression of exceptional depth and dimension. In the design the artist envisioned "great pine forests climbing huge mountains, higher and higher, until the climate restricts their growth. Mountain trails zigzag up the forested mountains, providing breathtaking rewards for the adventuresome soul." She notes that the design inspired her as she worked: "Working up the quilt I was like a mountain climber scaling a peak."

Nightshade resembles Rebecca's other quilts, but the color selection gave the artist some difficulty. The quilt expresses the lushness of a large garden, with entangling vines and seed pods that are about to burst. Rebecca wanted to reproduce a richly luxuriant feeling by using a variety of lights and darks from around the color wheel. Before she found the color combination that satisfied her and gave the intended message, Rebecca tested and discarded many colors and even changed two of them after the quilt pieces were cut. She says that it often takes her two or three days to pick colors for a quilt. She uses as many as 18 different colors in one quilt, and finding just the right grouping is not always a fast process.

Timberline; *57½ by 59¼ inches; cotton-blend chintz; machine pieced and hand quilted.*

Vineyard; *96 by 81 inches; cotton-blend chintz and tricot lamé; machine pieced and hand quilted.*

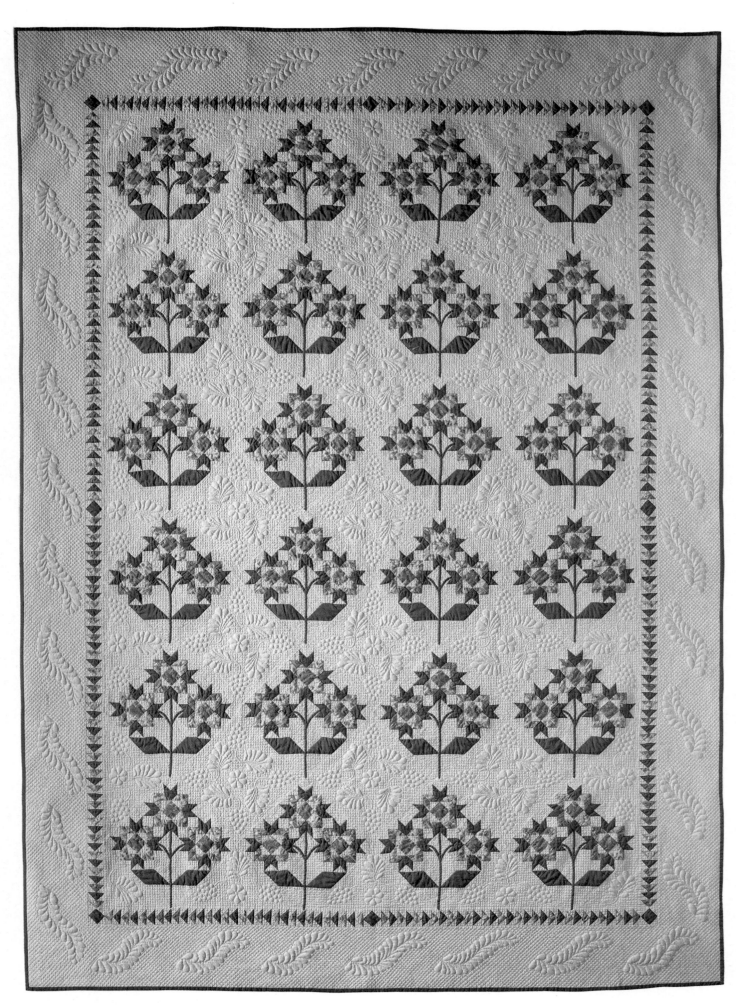

Lilies of the Field; *83 by 108 inches; all-cotton;*
hand pieced and hand quilted with trapunto.

BETTY EKERN SUITER

Betty Ekern Suiter first became interested in quilting when her mother gave her an unfinished Star pattern quilt top that had been rescued from her grandmother's attic. Who would have thought that this water-stained quilt top would inspire anyone? None of the fabrics complemented one another, there were not enough squares to make a quilt, and besides Betty did not even know how to quilt. Despite these obstacles, she was determined to make something beautiful. She washed the fabric, then she took the squares apart, put sashing in between them, and ended up with a 110-by-130-inch quilt top. When she finally began to quilt, she recalls laboriously stitching, using the punch-and-poke method and producing "uneven stitches with staggering, irregular lines." The end product was definitely not "quilt show material," she says, but her imagination had been challenged.

Betty's second quilt, *Cathedral Window*, was technically and aesthetically far more successful. Some thirty quilts later, Betty has won more than a hundred awards for her traditional quilts.

Betty relies on her training in mechanical drafting and seven years' experience as a draftsperson when she designs her quilts. While she was working out *Delectable Pansies*, the quiltmaker found that "the design just flowed onto the paper." An oriental rug was the original inspiration for the design, but the finished product looks nothing like the rug. The quilt is a bouquet of delicately hued pansies bound together with flowing pink ribbon. For this full-size appliquéd quilt, Betty dyed fabric to get the exact shades she wanted for her design. She also invented the feathered-spray quilting pattern, done in trapunto, that enhances the open spaces in the quilt.

The design for *Lilies of the Field* uses repeating patchwork blocks, each of which is composed of more than a hundred pieces, that are set on point alternately with trapunto blocks. The design for this quilt is deceptively simple. It is based on an 1850 New England quilt, but Betty did not want to mark the surface and she did not want needle marks to show on the back, so she marked the trapunto design on voile and used it to back the etched muslin top layer. She baste-quilted the design from the voile side, then did the trapunto before the blocks were assembled. After doing quarter-inch grid quilting over the muslin background, Betty removed the baste quilting with tweezers.

In a move away from traditional patterns, Betty created *Sharing Our Love Through the Seasons*. The thirteen counted cross-stitched blocks demanded intense concentration by the quilter, with the picture on each taking her about a month to complete. She chose polished cotton in shades of green for the sashing and border; the choice of colors creates a soothing effect, and the sheen of the cotton contrasts with the nonlustrous aida cloth that Betty used for her cross-stitched blocks.

Delectable Pansies, *72½ by 84 inches; all-cotton; appliquéd and hand quilted with trapunto.*

Sharing Our Love Through the Seasons *(detail)*.

Drunkard's Path; *86 by 110 inches; all-cotton;*
machine pieced and hand quilted.

SUSAN TURNER

Susan Turner adds new life and excitement to traditional patterns with fascinating color choices and her own unique arrangements. Susan has been sewing since she was ten years old, and in college she majored in home economics, concentrating on clothing and textiles. About twenty years ago, Susan bought a book of quilt patterns, and she says that it "was the beginning of cutting out little pieces and sewing them together." She taught herself how to piece and learned quilting by watching a group of quilters in Hot Springs, North Carolina, quilting around a large frame.

Susan made her first major quilt, which she called *Mushroom*, from Drunkard's Path pieces. She may spend anywhere from two months to well over a year on a quilt, depending on what else is going on in her life at the same time. *Tumbling Blocks*, for example, took about a year and a half, but the artist made it in spare moments while she and her husband were traveling in Asia. She felt that she was under some pressure to get all the blocks sewed together before they returned to the United States because she was afraid that once she was home she would not have the time to hand piece a quilt. She bought the fabric in India and drafted the pattern by experimenting with paper. "I love the optical illusion of the Tumbling Blocks design," she says, "and I saw many floor designs in Asia that reminded me of this pattern." She cut out pieces and sewed blocks while waiting for trains and buses, and then sewed away uncountable miles on long train rides. Piecing the quilt top attracted a lot of attention, and people everywhere were interested in what Susan was doing.

Drunkard's Path is a lovely traditional pattern that Susan enhanced with a pieced border that seems to echo the internal design. The artist chose to use a strong background color and a simple two-color path, giving this old favorite a modern, airy impression. Susan says that she likes the way the pattern pieces for this design look. She enjoyed stacking her fabric and cutting out eight or nine pieces at a time. The design also offers the challenge of sewing curves, but the artist says that this was not difficult for her.

A harmonious blend of lights and darks makes *Log Cabin* a truly elegant quilt. Susan pieced it like an old-fashioned scrap quilt, and it took her a couple of years to collect an assortment of fabrics large enough to give her the color combinations she wanted. "I tried to collect hundreds of different fabrics before I started to sew," she says. "Collecting fabric is a labor of love." Each of the 48 blocks that make up this quilt is different, and each is joined in a slightly different Log Cabin arrangement, giving the quilt overall an unusual sense of depth and dimension. The simple, decorative pattern of the border quilting sets off the colorful beauty of the center but does not detract from it.

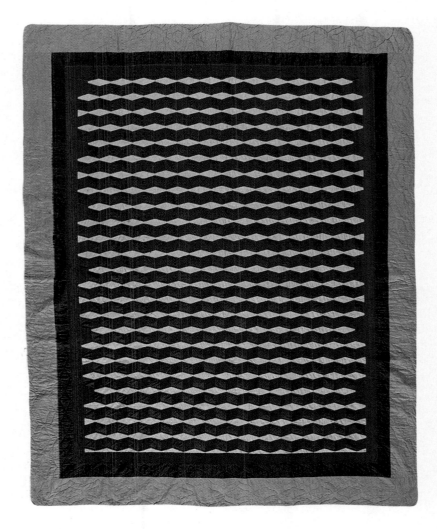

Tumbling Blocks; *90 by 112 inches; all-cotton; hand pieced and hand quilted.*

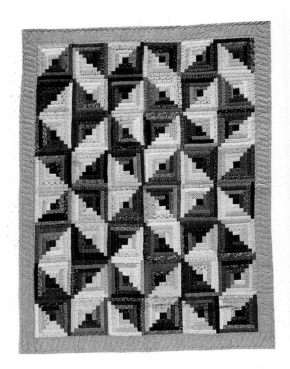

Log Cabin; *86 by 110 inches; all-cotton; machine pieced and hand quilted.*

Homage to Mondriaan I; *63 by 73 inches;*
all-cotton; machine pieced and machine quilted.

MEINY VERMAAS-VAN DER HEIDE

Meiny Vermaas-van der Heide satisfies her hunger for beauty, color, form, and texture through quilts that merge her Dutch heritage with the medium of American patchwork. Meiny learned to quilt in the Netherlands, but when she moved to the United States, she decided to take a closer look at the craft. She signed up for classes at a quilt shop. "I felt like a child again, having to relearn everything," she says, but quilting helped ease her transition to a new country by providing a focus for her energies as well as many new friends. Quilting, she notes, "was a vehicle that brought me into a new social network." Meiny also found that she learned a lot of American history by reading books about quilting.

Meiny now spends forty or fifty hours a week quilting. She believes that it is important to be organized in her work and to have the discipline to make time for quilting. She often works in design series and will make several tops and then quilt them consecutively. As she works, she focuses on the message she wants to get across with her quilt. "Being a foreigner in the U.S.A. I cannot vote, but I can still voice myself in my work," she says.

Positive/Negative is Meiny's original variation on the Dutchman's Puzzle pattern. It is a stark and dramatic image that is surprisingly complex. The pattern refers to Meiny's Dutch heritage, but the border points are a tribute to her mentor, Nancy Crow, who often uses points like these in her own work. She showed Meiny how to make them quickly. The artist chose to quilt in the ditch with invisible thread and used black thread in a striking sashiko pattern for the top, giving the quilt an extra element of intricacy.

Homage to Mondriaan I and *Homage to Mondriaan III* are part of a series of four quilts that were inspired by the work of the Dutch painter Pieter Mondriaan. In this series of quilts, Meiny refers to both the structure and the colors of his work. She explains that in his art Mondriaan was striving to find harmony within himself and with the surrounding world. In these quilts she is striving for harmony in the political world and in the environment.

In her first Mondriaan quilt, Meiny based her design on a variation of the traditional Triple Rail pattern. Because Mondriaan used large and uninterrupted plain spaces in his work, she decided to quilt only in the ditch. "I didn't want the surface to be interrupted with quilting lines," she says. The third quilt in the series is composed of black-and-white prints of differing values that encouraged Meiny to create the secondary pieced design that can be seen in the quilt top. This work was quilted more closely than the others because fabrics used in the top seemed to demand it.

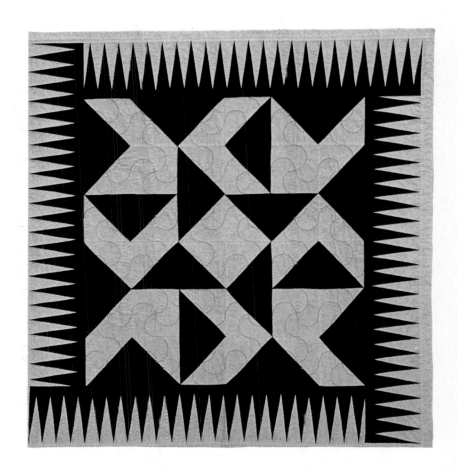

Positive/Negative; *43 by 43 inches; all-cotton; machine pieced and machine quilted.*

Homage to Mondriaan III; *63 by 63 inches; all-cotton; machine pieced and machine quilted.*

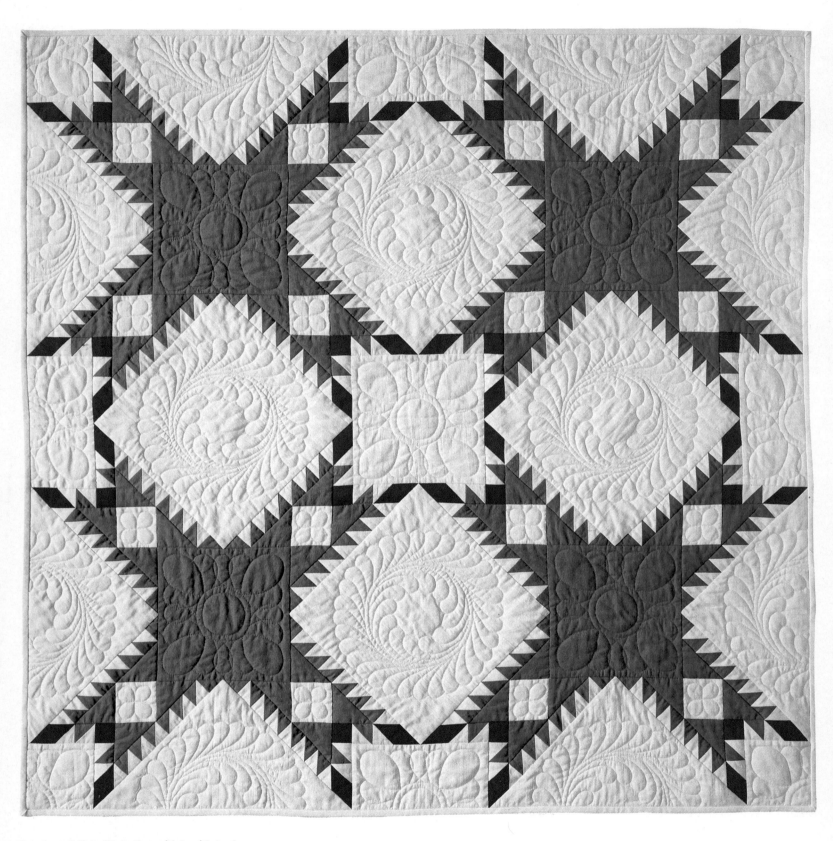

Feathered Star Variation; *41 by 41 inches;*
all-cotton; machine pieced and machine quilted.

DEBRA CHRISTINE WAGNER

Debra Christine Wagner has been making award-winning machine embroidery for 25 years. Her specialty is lace and cutwork. But a few years ago, she started quilting. It was a logical outgrowth of her interest in antique textiles, and a class in machine quilting, in which the teacher helped the students to recognize the inherent possibilities of this technique rather than its limitations, provided the final impetus. Machine quilting fits right in with the way Debra has blended other traditional needlework techniques and designs with the possibilities offered by modern technology.

The artist's first quilt was a simple four-inch square design called *Ceremonial Beads*, but much of her present work has been inspired by a fragment of an old trapunto quilt she owns. Using it as a pattern, Debra has recreated the hand stitching on her machine and substituted polyester fiberfill for yarn padding. The result is a spectacular machine-stitched trapunto quilt that pushes the limits of both design and technique into new realms.

Debra is drawn to the quilts made during the mid-nineteenth century that have strong graphic designs or exceptional quilting patterns. These quilts have inspired much of her work, although she varies the patterns slightly to reflect current tastes in symmetry and design. *Union Square* is a charming pieced wall hanging that is heavy with channel quilting and dramatic trapunto motifs. It was inspired by a quilt made in 1866 that is now in the Smithsonian Institution's collection. "I love the mathematical element of designing and executing the piecing," the artist says, "but I do find the actual quilting process boring at times and I have to exercise a great deal of self-discipline to keep at it."

Feathered Star Variation is a wall hanging based on a Scottish quilt made in 1833, which is itself a variation on the Feathered Star pattern. The Sawtooth piecing pattern and the small red inserts were a challenge for Debra because she did not want to interrupt the design with unnecessary seams. "I did have moments when I wondered if I'd get it all together," she says. Even though the quilting looks complex, the artist says that the original quilt had even more intricate stitching and she chose to simplify it somewhat so that the quilting would complement rather than compete with the piecing.

Double Nine Patch is a heavily quilted trapunto work with a design that is based on an antique quilt, which dates from around 1825 and is part of the Denver Art Museum's collection. Debra made this delightful and somewhat whimsical piece as a sampler to test the pattern and quilting design before she began making a full-size quilt. "This wall hanging was pure fun to do," she says. "I am looking forward to making the quilt."

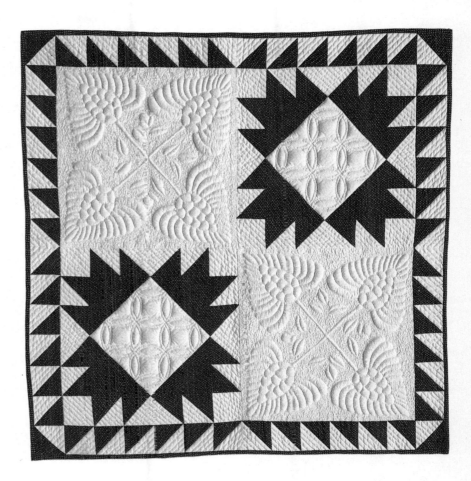

Union Square; *25½ by 25½ inches; all-cotton; machine pieced and machine quilted.*

Double Nine Patch; *19 by 19 inches; all-cotton; machine pieced and machine quilted.*

Pleasant Dreams; *94 by 108 inches; all-cotton;*
machine pieced and hand quilted.

GENEVA WATTS

Geneva Watts made her first quilt with her mother. She and her husband pieced her next quilt as a memorial to their daughter. In 1978 when Geneva became a full-time homemaker and her sister gave her a quilt that their mother was unable to finish, the artist began to quilt in earnest. She has made many quilts and wall hangings since then; some use traditional designs or are adaptations of traditional patterns, others are entirely her own, inspired by nature, art, and clothing designs. "I always have more designs developed than I have the time and opportunity to make," she says.

Prism Star has a bold, colorful centerpiece of eight pieced diamonds, set off by a dark ground. It is based on a Broken Star pattern. Geneva made this quilt in honor of the 37 foster babies that she and her husband have parented. When the babies were around three or four months old, they loved to watch the rainbows formed when the sun caught a crystal hanging in Geneva's window. The colors in the quilt are the same rainbow hues. The artist says that the quilt always reminds her of the joy the foster children brought her, of sunshine and laughter, and of eyes sparkling with love and delight.

Geneva used a traditional Lone Star pattern for *Pleasant Dreams*, which was a demonstration quilt for a class on making Lone Star quilts by the fast-piecing technique. The quilting in this piece is as spectacular as it is unusual, and it is totally the artist's creation. Although elaborate in concept and execution, the quilting plays off against the simplicity of the pieced central star and borders. Marking was a particularly time-consuming and difficult task for this complex design, since accuracy in stitching was crucial to the final effect. The carefully chosen gradations of color (11 shades of peach through deep rust were used) offset the richness of the design and help to make this a singularly restful quilt.

Quilting is Geneva Watts's occupation, and her time is scheduled accordingly. She averages forty to sixty hours a week on her work; occasionally deadlines push her workweek to seventy or more hours. Geneva is a certified quilt teacher and judge, but she believes that learning about quilts is a never-ending affair. She is still learning, experimenting, and attending workshops and lectures by today's important quilt teachers. Even though she recognizes the value of competition and enjoys winning, Geneva's real sense of satisfaction with quilting comes from within, from the knowledge that each quilt is a job well done.

Prism Star; *90 by 104 inches; all-cotton; machine pieced and hand quilted.*

Pleasant Dreams *(detail).*

Crazy Quilt #2; *42 by 60 inches; fiberglass,
computer-generated images on cotton rag paper,
silk thread, and paint; hand pieced and hand
quilted.*

CAROL D. WESTFALL

Carol D. Westfall has taken twentieth century technology and translated it into an exciting and lively application in her quilts, turning a traditional craft into contemporary art. Carol holds both undergraduate and graduate fine arts degrees with a special emphasis on textiles and has worked in a variety of fiber media for more than twenty years. She is a professor in the fiber program of the Fine Arts Department at Montclair State College in New Jersey. Quilting fits right in with Carol's work, but she has never limited herself to one medium for artistic expression. Carol has demonstrated her talent in structure and design through plaiting, weaving, and other fiber works for many years and has won much recognition through shows and publications.

The artist says that she seems to have been born sewing. She cannot remember when she did not know how to use a needle. Quilting is part of her family's needlework tradition, but she never did old-fashioned quilting. The inspiration to try her hand at a new aspect of this old craft came once she was teaching. Coupled with her long-standing fascination in the structure of woven fabrics, her reinterpretation of quilting produces highly unusual and dramatically different collage quilts.

Carol's quilts *Color Crazy Quilt, Crazy Quilt #1*, and *Crazy Quilt #2* translate the American Crazy Quilt tradition of the late-nineteenth century into a contemporary mode through her choice of materials and her use of technology. Carol relies on a computer to generate images based on fabric structures and patterns, such as twill, herringbone, tabby, and basket weave. She prints these images on paper that has a high rag content; "I use doctoral thesis paper," she says, "because it has the highest rag content (80 percent) that I can find, which makes it closest to cloth."

Carol rips the printed paper into random-width strips, and using a running stitch, she sews them onto a fiberglass screen with black silk thread. The artist leaves the ends of the stitches hanging loose so that they float across the top of the composition, adding texture and depth. In *Crazy Quilt #2* a welter of loose threads dominates the entire composition through which random spots of color glow. Carol paints colorful highlights on certain areas of her constructions. She gets shadowed effects by the way in which the imaged paper is layered onto the background screen, with the more heavily patterned images forming darker areas, as in *Color Crazy Quilt*. The heaviness or sparseness of the collage also adds to gradations of tone as in *Crazy Quilt #1*. "The whole process of making these quilts," says the artist, "is an unfolding, a joyous event for me."

Color Crazy Quilt; 42 by 60 inches; fiberglass, computer-generated images on cotton rag paper, silk thread, and paint; hand pieced and hand quilted.

Crazy Quilt #1; 42 by 60 inches; fiberglass, computer-generated images on cotton rag paper, silk thread, and paint; hand pieced and hand quilted.

Amish Spring with Feathers and Lace; *89 by 89 inches (includes lace edging); all-cotton; machine pieced and hand quilted with trapunto.*

182

BEVERLY MANNISTO WILLIAMS

For Beverly Mannisto Williams an open space on a quilt top is "like a playground to a child." She likes nothing better than to fill the area with intricate and delicate patterns that both please and amaze. Beverly is known for her superlative quilting, but she is also able to create exquisite handmade lace edgings for quilts and has a wonderful sense of color and design. "I have always loved to sew, ever since I was very young," she says, "and finally I decided to put my energy into some major efforts that would provide lasting results rather than everyday disposable projects." There is no doubt that her lovely quilts are likely to be treasured for many years to come.

Beverly's first quilt was a traditional Grandmother's Flower Garden design, and she has since made many wall hangings and five full-size quilts, two of which have won major awards. Her designs come from books, advertisements, nature, and her love for certain shapes, including ovals, plumes, and anything with the possibility of adding feathering. She has been quilting and making lace for about ten years and has given up most of her other needlework activities so she can concentrate on these two. "I am so lucky to have found these two interests," she says. "The more I am involved in it, the more I love the process."

Amish Spring with Feathers and Lace combines Beverly Williams's favorite skills with her favorite shapes in a magnificent award-winning quilt that is the perfect showcase for her considerable talent. The pieced top, executed in soft pastels, uses a simple and traditional Amish Diamond in a Square pattern. The quilting design is a complex original compendium of feathery plumes, medallions, rosettes, hearts, bows, and shell shapes with trapunto added to give a more sculptured effect. The two-and-a-half-inch bobbin-lace edging, which Beverly hand made specifically for this quilt, carries out and accentuates the elements of the quilted design.

When she began this quilt, the artist estimated that it could take her as long as five years to finish it, given the detail and complexity of the overall design. But she completed the quilt in only 15 months because she enjoyed working on it so much. For her, the quilting, which took about 2500 hours, and the bobbin lace which required another 325 hours, represent patience and peace of mind in an otherwise fast-moving and disposable society.

Because she has a part-time job selling fabrics, Beverly cannot always find as much time to quilt and make lace as she would like. "I try to have one day a week for an all-day quilting binge, then I work in whatever other moments are available—and sometimes it's hard to pull myself away from my projects to take care of other matters in life." She says she is a very slow quilter, but she is never in a hurry. Beverly's only concern is doing the best job she can.

Amish Spring with Feathers and Lace *(detail)*.

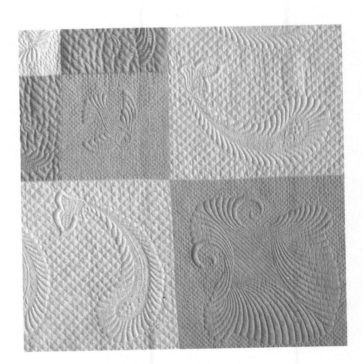

Amish Spring with Feathers and Lace *(detail)*.

ERMA MARTIN YOST

Cloud Catcher; *27¹/₂ by 27¹/₂ inches; cotton, cotton blends, hand-printed fabric, synthetic metallic fabrics and thread, yucca leaves, and willow twigs; machine pieced and machine quilted. Collection of Michael and Taylor Lupica.*

Cumulus I; *54 by 40 inches; cotton and artist's linen; machine pieced, appliquéd, machine quilted, and tied. Collection of Chicopee, Inc.*

Cumulus II; *54 by 40 inches; cotton, linen, and synthetic metallic fabrics; machine pieced, appliquéd, machine quilted, and tied. Collection of Chicopee, Inc.*

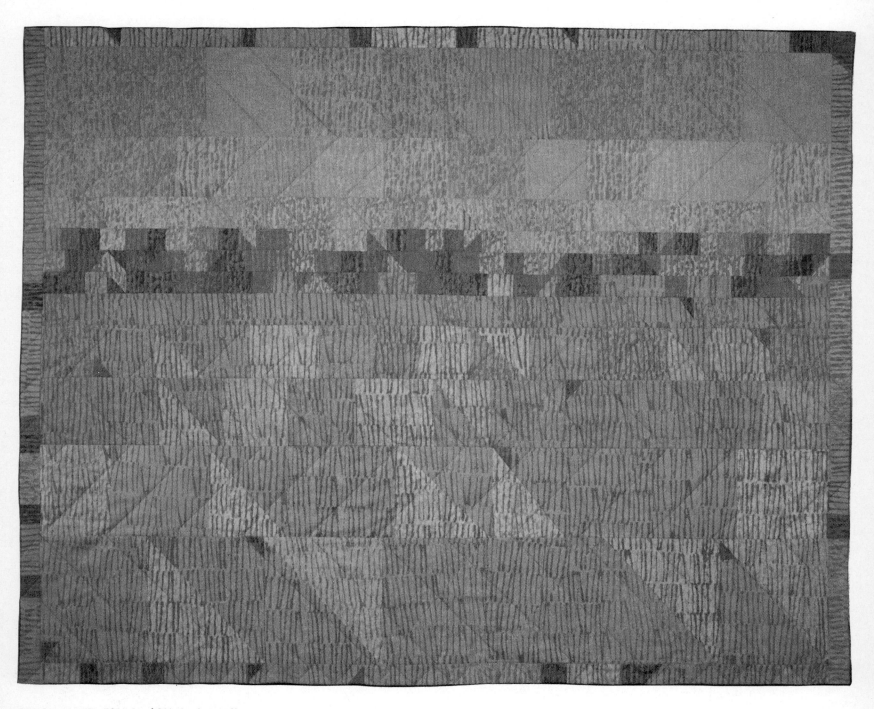

Landscape #5; *53¹/₂ by 42¹/₂ inches; all-cotton;
machine pieced and machine quilted.*

EMILY ZOPF

Abstract landscapes are the subject of Emily Zopf's quilts. Her surroundings are the basis for her designs. The artist's mother, who is also a quilter, encouraged her daughter's interest and taught her the basics of the craft. Emily has learned the rest of what she knows about quilting from extensive reading and trial and error. Her first quilt was a Chinese Coin pattern made in wool, and she has since made more than forty quilts.

To get the subtle results that the artist prefers for her pictorial abstractions, she hand prints many of her fabrics. Her technique produces an unusual impression of shading. She wraps twine around a block of wood that she uses as a printing template and then prints each color of fabric with two or more colors of paint from the template, creating the effect of graduated color changes from one quilt piece to the next.

Emily's quilt *Grass and Rain* is a yellow field against a brilliant blue sky. On her daily commute, the artist sometimes passes through a similar scene when the sun washes a field with color at the same time that rain continues to fall. The vertical printing of the fabric denotes both rain in the sky and grass in the field; the horizon line becomes diffused as the golds and blues of the fabrics blend together. Emily spent a long time researching the color combinations for this quilt, but the end result is a celebration of the pleasure that she gets from viewing the landscape around her.

Landscape with Houses is a combination of patchwork and appliqué that was inspired by the land near the artist's home and by "the similarity between places and lifestyles around the world," Emily says. The vertical printing of the fabric enhances the feeling of space, distance, and extensive grassy fields, while overlapped zigzag quilting adds a textural element as well as a sense of movement. "There were times," says the artist, "when I was frustrated during the design process. I made many changes in the look and placement of the houses in particular."

Landscape #5 ties the neat geometry of Midwest farmland to a dark line of trees and buildings on a far horizon. In addition to the landscape, an African textile inspired Emily to design this quilt in which the pieces become smaller as they reach the horizon to produce a sense of perspective and depth. The widely spaced zigzag quilting highlights the diagonals of the fields and helps move the eye toward the horizon line. "Not knowing how the pieces would look when they were put together and then having to make changes so the composition works" was the difficult part of this quilt, the artist says.

Emily, who holds a master's degree in fiber arts, currently works full time as a quilter. Depending on the complexity of design and the size of the quilt, she may spend anywhere from a month to a few months completing a quilt.

Skyline Quilt; *74 by 51 inches; all-cotton; machine pieced and machine quilted.*

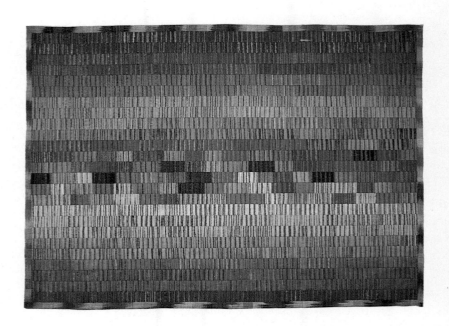

Grass and Rain; *52 by 37 inches; all-cotton; machine pieced and machine quilted.*

EMILY ZOPF

Landscape with Houses; *63 by 38 inches;
all-cotton; machine pieced, appliquéd, and
machine quilted.*

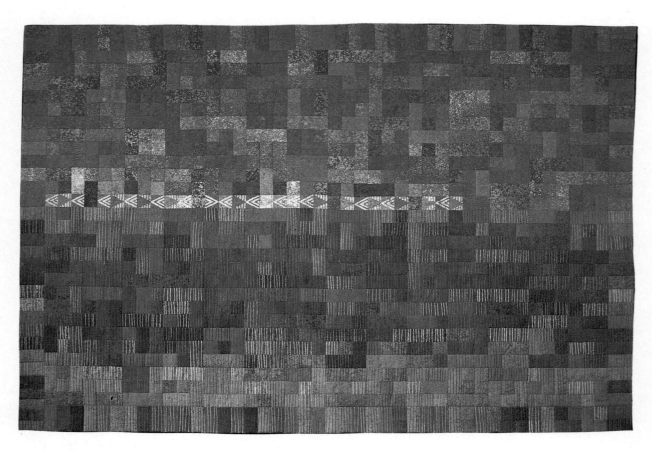

Landscape; *66 by 44 inches; all-cotton; machine
pieced and machine quilted.*

GLOSSARY

Appliqué: stitching a fabric cutout design onto background fabric.

Bargello: a needlepoint stitch that produces a zigzag pattern.

Block: a unit of a quilt top made up of patchwork or appliqué.

Broderie perse: "Persian embroidery," chintz appliqué designs.

Echo quilting: stitching that follows the contour of appliqué or patchwork in evenly spaced rows.

English paper piecing: basting fabric shapes to slightly smaller pieces of paper of the same shape, turning under the fabric edges, and then joining the pieces together with whip stitches.

Fan quilting: a stitching pattern of concentric arcs, or fans.

Fraktur: Pennsylvania Dutch decorative calligraphy.

Meander quilting: rows of contour quilting worked very close together.

Ogee: a pointed arch.

Piecing: sewing together patchwork pieces.

Quilting in the ditch: outline stitching along patchwork seams.

Reverse appliqué: basting together several layers of fabric and then cutting away areas of the top layers to expose a design.

Sashing: strips of fabric stitched between quilt blocks.

Seminole patchwork: a piecing technique developed by the Seminole Indians of southern Florida in which strips of fabric are stitched together, cut across, turned around, and rejoined to produce geometric patterns.

Stipple quilting: rows of contour quilting worked very close together.

String piecing: joining narrow strips of fabric.

Template piecing: another name for English paper piecing.

Trapunto: adding extra stuffing to a quilted or appliquéd design.

Tying: securing the layers of a quilt with embroidery floss or yarn.

Whole-cloth quilt: a quilt top made of solid-color fabric.

Harriet Powers, The Creation of the Animals, *1898; 105 by 69 inches; cotton and metallic yarn; hand pieced, appliquéd, and hand quilted.*

ACKNOWLEDGMENTS

Amish Country Collection
New Castle, Pennsylvania

Jennifer Amor
Columbia, South Carolina

Appalachian Fireside Crafts
Berea, Kentucky

Judy Becker
Newton, Massachusetts

Sue Benner
Dallas, Texas

Tafi Brown
Alstead, New Hampshire

Betty Jo Bucich
Glen Burnie, Maryland

Carol E. Butzke
Slinger, Wisconsin

Joyce Marquess Carey
Madison, Wisconsin

Barbara Lydecker Crane
Lexington, Massachusetts

Michael Cummings
New York, New York

Judy Dales
Boonton Township, New Jersey

Nancy Brenan Daniel
Tempe, Arizona

Chris Wolf Edmonds
Lawrence, Kansas

Ann Fahl
Racine, Wisconsin

Caryl Bryer Fallert
Oswego, Illinois

Marianne Fons
Winterset, Iowa

Pat Brooks Gaska
Rothschild, Wisconsin

Helen Giddens
Mesquite, Texas

Hope Green
Miami, Florida

Rosie Grinstead
Mission Hills, Kansas

Jane Hall
Raleigh, North Carolina

Barbara Oliver Hartman
Flower Mound, Texas

Dixie Haywood
Pensacola, Florida

Esther A. Hershberger
Goshen, Indiana

Mary Kay Hitchner
Haverford, Pennsylvania

Lois K. Ide
Bucyrus, Ohio

Damaris Jackson
Minneapolis, Minnesota

Ann Joyce
Columbus, Ohio

Natasha Kempers-Cullen
Bowdoinham, Maine

Helen King
Cave Creek, Arizona

Ann Kowaleski
Mt. Pleasant, Michigan

Judith Larzelere
Dedham, Massachusetts

Emiko Toda Loeb
New York, New York

Linda R. MacDonald
Willits, California

Jan Maher
Greensboro, North Carolina

Marguerite Malwitz
Brookfield, Connecticut

Merrill Mason
Jersey City, New Jersey

Judy Mathieson
Woodland Hills, California

Therese May
San Jose, California

Margaret J. Miller
Woodinville, Washington

Judith Montaño
Castle Rock, Colorado

Joanne F. Moulden
Berkeley Springs, West Virginia

Clare M. Murray
Canton, Ohio

Jan Myers-Newbury
Pittsburgh, Pennsylvania

Miriam Nathan-Roberts
Berkeley, California

Julia Overton Needham
Knoxville, Tennessee

Velda E. Newman
Nevada City, California

Ruth M. Norton
Rochester, New York

Ellen Oppenheimer
Oakland, California

Cherry Partee
Edmonds, Washington

Katie Pasquini
Oxnard, California

Linda S. Perry
Lexington, Massachusets

Barbara Rickey
Bellevue, Washington

Joan M. Rigal
Waterville, Ohio

Kathryn Rouse
Racine, Wisconsin

Rose Sanders
Covington, Louisianna

Stephanie Santmyers
Greensboro, North Carolina

Jane A. Sassaman
Chicago, Illinois

Robin Schwalb
Brooklyn, New York

Susan Shie
Wooster, Ohio

Rebekka Siegel
Owenton, Kentucky

Elly Sienkiewicz
Washington, D.C.

Lois Tornquist Smith
Rockville, Maryland

Smokey Mountain Quilters
Knoxville, Tennessee

Rebecca Speakes
Minneapolis, Minnesota

Betty Ekern Suiter
Racine, Wisconsin

Susan Turner
Asheville, North Carolina

Meiny Vermaas-van der Heide
Tempe, Arizona

Debra Christine Wagner
Hutchinson, Minnesota

Geneva Watts
Racine, Wisconsin

Carol D. Westfall
Nutley, New Jersey

Beverly Mannisto Williams
Cadillac, Michigan

Erma Martin Yost
Jersey City, New Jersey

Emily Zopf
Seattle, Washington